Basalt Regional Library
99 Midland Avenue
Basalt CO 81621
927-4311

RISKING
ADVENTURE

MOUNTAINEERING
JOURNEYS
AROUND
THE WORLD

Jim Haberl

RAINCOAST BOOKS

Vancouver

First published in 1997 by

Raincoast Books
8680 Cambie Street
Vancouver, B.C.
V6P 6M9
(604) 323-7100

1 2 3 4 5 6 7 8 9 10

CANADIAN CATALOGUING IN PUBLICATION DATA

Haberl, Jim, 1958-
Risking adventure

(Raincoast journeys)
ISBN 1-55192-093-X

1. Haberl, Jim, 1958- – Journeys. 2. Mountaineering. 3.
Mountaineering – Psychological aspects. I. Title. II. Series.
GV199.92.H32A3 1997   796.5'22'092   C97-910399-1

Designed by Dean Allen
Edited by Michael Carroll

Printed and bound in Singapore

*Raincoast Books gratefully acknowledges the support of the Canada
Council, the Department of Canadian Heritage, and the
British Columbia Arts Council.*

TITLE PAGE: *Jim Brennan jumars the wildly exposed tyrolean traverse from the Lost Arrow Spire back to the main rim of Yosemite
Valley in California. The crashing flow of water in the background is
the thunderous explosion of Upper Yosemite Falls.*

To Sue, my partner in the biggest adventure of all – life

CONTENTS

*Eric Boyum rappels through an icefall on the Scimitar
Glacier in the Waddington Range, British Columbia.*

FOREWORD

I FIRST MET JIM HABERL by way of a phone call back in the fall of 1993. He had recently returned from a tumultuous expedition during which he had reached the summit of the beautiful and forbidding mountain, K2. All had not gone well on that climb: Jim's close friend Dan Culver had lost his life shortly after he and Jim had stood together on top of the world's second-highest peak. The accomplishment was a first for Canadians and a personal highlight for Jim, but his friend's death had tarnished the entire experience. I phoned Jim as a reporter, writing an assignment for *Outside* magazine about the events of that fateful summer on K2, during which many climbers had died.

Initially Jim was suspicious of my phone call. No doubt he wondered, who is this stranger calling to ask about a part of my life that is a perplexing mixture of glowing epiphany and heart-rending tragedy? But he knew I was a climber who had also climbed K2, and we spoke for a long time, less about the details of his expedition and more about the mysterious nature of that strange need we climbers have to venture into wild, sometimes dangerous places.

Jim and I have had occasional meetings since that time, and the discussion we began that day on the phone after his K2 expedition has often been the stuff of our conversations. The question Jim asks himself in *Risking Adventure* is this: why do we venture out into the wildest of places, away from the warmth and security of our safe existences in the cities? And why do we embark on that dangerous path when we know that a safe path could be followed?

As an accomplished mountaineer, rock climber, guide, wilderness skier, and backwoodsman, Jim has put himself in a lot of wild places both for the fun of it and for the self-enlightenment that such experiences offer. He does not claim to

Keith Reid crests the knife-edge at 10,800 feet on the unclimbed Southeast Ridge of Mount St. Elias, Alaska.

have figured out with finality the answer to the irritating question of why we under-take the perilous journey, but neither has anyone else. By asking the question, though, and by describing those electrifying and even terrifying moments on a mountain when the elements conspire against you, Jim has tabled the enigmatic question of "why" for discussion. His skills as a photographer add depth to his words, and his experiences on mountains, rivers, and snowcaps are written in straightforward language that is as clear as an alpine stream. This book is far more than a climber's memoir: it is Jim's attempt to understand his own hunger for adventure.

Greg Child
1997

ACKNOWLEDGMENTS

HUNDREDS OF FRIENDS and acquaintances supported and bought my first book, *K2: Dreams and Reality*. Thank you. Because of your encouragement this second effort seemed worth trying.

Risking Adventure was only possible with the assistance that I continue to receive from my friends and family. For their dedicated efforts in reading various parts of the manuscript and offering their thoughts, I would like to thank my mother, Margaret Haberl; my brothers, Pat and Kevin; Kevin's wife, Vicki; my sister, Sue Pendakur, Alan Greer; Dave and Debbie Freeze; Matt and Chris MacEachern; Peter and Liz Mair; Mike White and Rose Johnson; Keith Reid; Julia Taffe; Rob Rohn and Julie Timmins; and Michael Down.

My dad, Bill Haberl, took great care in reading and offering his editorial comments with each draft version of the entire book – no easy task. Vic Marks, Rob Orvig, Bob Herger, Alastair Foreman, and Phil Powers all contributed in different ways to the project. Greg Child kindly agreed to write a foreword, then waited patiently for six months between broken promises for the manuscript. Michael Carroll, Dean Allen, Mark Stanton, and the staff at Raincoast Books took an early interest and stuck with the project along the potholed road this book has traveled. And a very special thanks goes out to Sue Oakey, who supports who I am and gives me perspective.

Introduction

ADVENTURE. Simply writing the word brings images of unique situations, exciting moments, and unfamiliar places to mind. By committing to an adventure, stepping out of my comfort zone, I accept that unforeseeable things are bound to happen. For me, that unknown element is a large part of the attraction of any trip. While it is true that unknown circumstances may be arduous, stressful, or even dangerous, I learn important things about myself by contending with and surviving those events.

Just as often, though less dramatic and more difficult to express, by exposing myself to such dynamic situations I experience beautiful, sometimes extraordinary, moments. Those moments could not have been part of my life if I hadn't accepted the risk of following the passion in my heart.

Risk is the process of engaging in an activity without the security of knowing the consequences of your decision. When I set out to climb a mountain, there is a powerful appeal based on the uncertainty of the outcome. If it were a sure thing, then the attraction would diminish. Periodically I take a calculated risk, relying on my seasoning as a mountaineer and my intuition – many treasured experiences are the result of such decisions. Yet learning to recognize when something is unsafe or beyond my control has been a critical lesson. To retreat in the face of danger, suppressing ambition, is not only wise, it is admirable.

There is nothing more rewarding than taking a risk and succeeding. This is a crucial element in the development of risk tolerance. Climbing a mountain and safely reaching the summit generates self-confidence that is based on experience

I

Michael Down front points up steep spring ice on the
Weeping Wall in the Canadian Rockies.

and competence. But success is intoxicating, and each accomplishment is merely a milestone on a longer journey. Look around and you will see that prosperous people crave more of whatever it was that made them successful. Committed athletes risk their bodies regularly and consciously sacrifice other aspects of their lives to excel at their craft, and still have difficulty retiring. Not because they need another year's salary or other perks that may come their way, but more likely because their sport has provided them with a powerful sense of identity and personal worth.

When effective businesspeople achieve financial independence, usually through a combination of hard work and shrewd management, it is rare to see them retire. The potency of their personalities is wrapped up in the challenge, the excitement, and the potential for failure or achievement. In my case, having once tasted the freedom, the demands, and the incredible rewards of mountaineering, the desire to go again was inevitable.

To attempt such a venture and fail comes with a cost, but to dream of something within my means and never to pursue that dream exacts an even greater price. We grow as individuals as we explore and extend our personal boundaries.

People often tell me that I'm lucky, that I lead an unusual and adventurous life. My customary response to such a comment is that I know I'm fortunate, but I have also worked very hard at my chosen direction. I enjoy guiding and climbing mountains and I wouldn't trade those experiences for anything. Yet, like everyone I know, many aspects of my day-to-day life contain fragile uncertainties. Will I find enough work next month to pay the rent? Can Sue and I raise a family and still maintain an adventurous lifestyle? Should we stay in the city or move to a rural setting? In short, one of my life's biggest challenges is determining the best way to answer a multitude of "ordinary" questions.

What has helped provide the means for me to grow as an individual has been my exposure to our natural environment. By testing myself on the great mountains of the world, I am better prepared for the many challenges in my life. Mountain climbing is dramatic and decisions can sometimes mean life or death. But even in everyday life we make decisions that can change the entire course of our careers or personal development. This book explores the notion that risk, and adventure, need to be part of all of our lives.

*Keith Reid jamming neatly up The Sword on the
Grand Wall at Squamish, British Columbia.*

The Burden of Risk
Tragedy on K2

The cold Vancouver rain bounces off the asphalt, blurring the headlights of passing cars. I stand outside the high school auditorium gathering my thoughts and wondering how many people will show up on this miserable December night. It is going to be a tough evening for me. For the first time I will show these slides and share the whole story.

Five months have passed since our team climbed K2, but the experience is still fresh in my mind. Occasionally my thoughts dwell on our achievement and the incredible adventure we experienced on that mountain, but usually I think about Dan. Sometimes I try to picture what happened, a process that always leads to the same question: Why did he fall? Most other times I try to imagine what it would be like if he were alive. It is still easy to cry, but that is gradually changing.

Time really does heal.

Now, as I watch the rain pummel the pavement, I shiver with each gust of icy wind and find my mind slipping back once again to that unforgettable expedition. The memories are like shards of broken glass . . .

OUR TEAM – Stacy Allison, John Petroske, Phil Powers, John Haigh, Steve Steckmyer, Dan Culver, and myself – arrives in Pakistan on May 23 and spends more than two weeks traveling through the country to the base of K2, the world's second highest and, arguably, most notorious peak. First climbed in 1954 by a strong Italian team, its elusive summit has been attained by fewer than 90 people. For nine days

5

The enormous South Face of K2 viewed from Concordia, the junction of the Baltoro and Godwin-Austen Glaciers. The huge amphitheater was named by British explorer Martin Conway, the leader of the first mountaineering expedition to visit the heart of the Baltoro region.

of those first two weeks we travel on foot, trekking into the mountains with the two and a half tonnes of food and equipment we will need for 10 weeks above 5,000 meters in the Himalayas. We employ 107 porters to help us with that task. Then, after establishing base camp on the glacier beneath the mammoth South Face, we spend the next month working on the mountain, carrying loads and establishing camps on the steep Abruzzi Ridge, preparing K2 and ourselves for a summit attempt.

We choose to climb K2 without the aid of bottled oxygen, striving to meet the mountain on its own terms. After all, its great height is possibly its best defense. Because of this choice, our bodies need time to adapt to the thin air of extreme altitude, an acclimatization process that takes weeks. We heed the unwritten rules, taking the necessary time and moving slowly up the mountain, learning the route and anchoring ropes to facilitate going up and, more important, to provide for a quick escape in the face of bad weather. After each foray, we return to base camp to recover. When the next good weather occurs, we go back to the mountain and attempt to climb higher. By the end of June we are ready to dare for the top.

More than 100 porters wait patiently for their loads to be packed on the morning of June 3, 1993, at Paiju. This camp marks the halfway point of the 10-day approach to K2. From Paiju the trail leaves the Braldu River Valley and climbs onto the toe of the Baltoro Glacier.

PHIL, DAN, AND I ARE CHOSEN by Stacy, our team leader, to be the first summit team. When she announces her decision, I am electrified by the prospect of going for the top. My imagination shifts to the mountain, and I have a clear picture of myself standing on the summit.

At 2:30 a.m. on June 29 we leave base camp at 5,000 meters, hoping to reach camp 2 that day. Storms have lashed the mountain for four days, depositing 50 centimeters of fresh snow. We take turns breaking trail, lifting the fixed ropes out of the snow, and making footsteps for the others to follow. The climbing is strenuous. Twelve hours later we cram ourselves into our small tent at 6,700 meters and begin the tedious ritual of melting snow for water.

Sunset is breathtaking. At camp 2 we are already higher than most peaks of the Karakoram, an impressive chain of mountains that nature has placed parallel to the main sweep of the greater Himalayas. The Karakoram contains five peaks rising to a height of more than 8,000 meters; only 14 mountains on the planet are that high. As the sun dips to the horizon, it produces a warm orange glow on the peaks to the east. I watch Phil take a last look around before he zips the tent door. Camp 2 is left in the deep blue shadows cast by the mass of the mountain above. We burrow into our thick down sleeping bags to insulate ourselves against the plummeting temperatures.

It is an agonizingly uncomfortable night. Phil is crammed against the uphill wall of the tent, Dan is tight against the downhill side, and I am in the middle. A movement by one is immediately felt by the others. At different times we each wake to pee in the tiny bottles we carry for that purpose. The ensuing gymnastics inside the sleeping bag to make sure there are no spills or overflows further disrupts our night. Going outside would be very cold and the risk of a slip on the icy slopes too real to ignore. Every distraction costs us sleep. And, besides the physical discomforts, I am suffering from congestion in my lungs that keeps me awake most of the night. In the morning we all look worn out as we prepare to move on to camp 3 and, with luck, to the summit of K2.

My climb to camp 3 proves difficult. I feel terrible and move slowly. I am nauseous, my breathing is labored, and my head aches. Our packs have all the equipment needed for an attempt on the summit: sleeping bags, tents, stoves, and food.

FOLLOWING PAGES: *Sunset on the West Face of Masherbrum, Karakoram Range, Pakistan. At 7,821 meters above sea level, Masherbrum is the 30th highest peak in the world.*

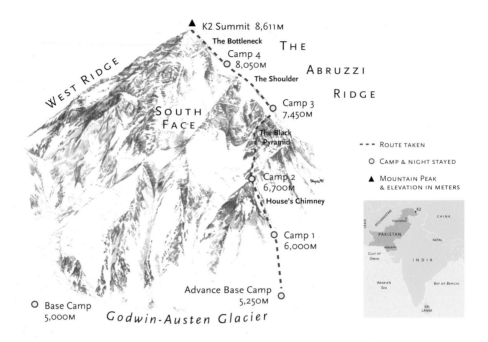

Mine weighs more than 15 kilograms, too heavy for my present condition. I strug-gle with the effort. The congestion in my chest makes me question if going up was the right decision.

One's reasons for climbing a peak like K2 are intensely personal. To know if you can do it is a question that can only be answered by trying. The challenge, the stark beauty of the environment, sharing with partners the demands of a moun-tain of K2's stature, ambition, exploring the unknown, adventure – all these rea-sons and many more only begin to answer the ultimate question: Why? And there is no denying the risk. Of the hundreds of climbers who try, only a few reach the top. For every 10 people who achieve the summit of K2, four die somewhere on the mountain. Most die on summit day in the extreme altitudes above 8,000 meters. Yet to achieve that summit . . .

As I fight to keep pace with Dan and Phil, I know my chance for the top might be slipping away. I continue up slowly for an hour, agonizing over my fading prospect. Gradually I convince myself that retreat is the right decision, that it isn't just a case of my giving up in the face of hardship.

Phil Powers, with a load destined for camp 1, climbs on the fixed lines. The crevasses of the Godwin-Austen Glacier are evident 750 meters below.

"Dan!" I yell to catch the attention of my friends. "Phil!" They both turn and look at me from above. "I'm going back to camp 2. I can't do it." I hate to say the words, but I know it is the honest thing to do.

"Are you sure?" Dan shouts back. "We can take some of the stuff out of your pack if that will help."

"No, I'm really struggling. You guys go on." They are climbing strongly, and to have me along, coughing and fighting with the altitude, might ruin their chances for the top. It is clear to me that I'm not ready. My body needs more time. "Good luck, you guys. Be careful up there." I want them to reach the top. I only wish I could be there to share it. With regret, I set up my descender and rappel back to camp 2, while Dan and Phil turn and continue up toward camp 3 in the sunshine.

Now, alone at camp 2 on a beautiful afternoon, I decide to stay on the mountain and persevere with my acclimatization process. Staying high will give my body a chance to get used to the extreme elevation. Going back to base camp will mean giving up completely. Another night of acclimatization at 6,700 meters will help my chance for the summit. Our team still has six weeks left on K2 before the brutal storms of winter will arrive.

I set to work carving a platform out of the rock and ice so that we can pitch a second shelter. I know the rest of our team is on its way up to camp 2, carrying another tent, which will require a site. The light activity makes me breathe hard, but I feel stronger as the day progresses. I begin to feel better about my decision to wait, knowing that going up the mountain before the body is ready can be a serious mistake. My partners eventually arrive from below and help with the task. Once the second tent is up, we move inside for the night.

Dan and Phil were unable to find our team's cache of food and fuel at camp 3 and, with night approaching and no stove or food, they made the wise decision to abandon their first attempt. At 7:00 p.m., just before dark, they rappel into camp 2. The rest of the team is already comfortably settled for the night. The weather has begun to deteriorate, and with our two tiny tents full, Dan and Phil choose to continue their descent to base camp. The next morning those of us still in camp 2 awake to blowing snow and a falling barometer. Retreat is the only safe strategy, and by lunch on July 1 the entire team is safely in base camp. Confronting bad weather high on K2 is to tempt death. It was time to rest in base camp.

Besides skill and experience, the great mountains of the world demand an incredible amount of patience. That virtue must then be blended judiciously with enthusiasm. You need patience with the weather, patience with conditions on the route, and patience with your mind-set – and then the enthusiasm and teamwork to be able to strike when the situation for an ascent presents itself. Achieving that merger is a delicate challenge. By their very nature, patience and enthusiasm are at odds. Determining the opportune moment for a summit bid is equally difficult, and on K2 such moments rarely occur. If a chance does arise, the sinister weather ensures that it is brief.

Dan works his way up fixed ropes toward camp 1 during a snowstorm.

As the morning of July 2 unfolds, clouds stream over the summit and snow begins to fall. Inside my tent, lying in my sleeping bag, I stare at the nylon ceiling and speculate when our next chance at the mountain will come. A violent bout of coughing overtakes me as I lie there, and I uncomfortably discharge thick phlegm from the depths of my chest.

The thin, dry air of this altitude has taken its toll, and I wonder if I have either the ability or the conviction to pursue a mountain like K2. This is my first Himalayan peak. Am I being honest with myself? With my teammates? Tired and discouraged, I close my eyes and try to expel the negative thoughts.

"How's it going in there, Jim?" It's Dan. His question breaks my spell of reflection. "Lunch is ready and, man, is it snowing out here!"

"Thanks. I'll be there in a minute."

I pull on my snow boots and down parka and crawl out of the tent Dan and I are sharing in base camp. I turn my shoulder to the frigid wind blowing up the glacier. There is already 10 centimeters of fresh snow on the ground.

The slide show is scheduled for 7:30 p.m., and people begin to arrive an hour early. Everyone is anxious to get out of the rain, but by seven o'clock there is such a crowd outside that it is hard to get through the doors. I watch as people move inside, lowering their umbrellas and flipping back the hoods of their parkas. I recognize so many faces: family members, old friends, 20 years' worth of climbing partners. It seems that all of the people in my life are here.

By the time the first slide hits the giant screen, there are 1,000 people crammed into the auditorium, every seat is taken, and many audience members are standing in the aisles. More than 200 people have been turned away at the door.

Words don't come easily at first. I begin with images of my climbing partners from past trips, friends on journeys who helped shape and condition me for my chance to climb K2. I become emotional immediately, realizing how vital my friends are to me. When the shot of my brothers on top of Alaska's Denali 10 years earlier fills the screen, I find it difficult to fight back tears of pride.

Then I move to the K2 story and introduce our team. The first slide is a shot of Dan. I stare out into the audience, knowing that his wife, Patti, and her son, Ryan, are there. When I returned to Canada, Dan's family and friends wanted to know why he didn't come home. Now I try to speak, but a surge of emotion constricts my throat and chokes off my words.

I press the button in my hand, and Dan's image fades. Anyone who doesn't know him before tonight will come to understand his amazing qualities as the evening unfolds. Stacy's face fills the screen, and words of admiration for her strength and effort on K2 come easily. The pictures of my teammates bring back fond memories of each one, and warm introductions flow naturally. Soon the story is under way, and my tale of the long approach and struggle on the mountain pours out. It feels great to relive the journey.

There is so much to tell. Each day of our trip had special moments. Every slide sparks memories. Passionately I try to detail everything. I want everyone to know the joys and frustrations we felt in Pakistan. It is important to me that everyone comes to understand how well our team performed. I want them to gain an appreciation of what our ambitions were on K2 and how that journey played a vital part in each of our lives.

Why would anyone go to a place like K2 and gamble with the prospect of the unknown, the possible loss of toes or fingers to frostbite, and the ever-present reality of death? On the face of it, I have no answer. Logically mountaineering is a senseless game, particularly when viewed through the double-paned, tinted window of our comfortable and safe society. Often enough, society is determined to answer all my questions, removing from me the need to accept responsibility for my actions and for life's inherent risks. So the question, why climb a mountain like K2, becomes a private one; difficult to answer with enough clarity to satisfy myself, let alone the people trying to understand my motives. Yet for me, and many others, there is a powerful need to attempt, to explore the boundaries of what is possible. Without striving to go beyond what I already know I can attain, without stepping outside that zone of comfort in which I exist from day to day, there is no growth.

One by one my slides fill the screen, each image dissolving smoothly into

15

FOLLOWING PAGES: *Despite its dramatic relief, the sheer Nameless Tower, one of the many granite spires that rise thousands of meters above the Baltoro Glacier, is tucked with seeming insignificance beside its dominant neighbor, the Great Trango Tower.*

the next. The long approach ends and we begin our efforts on the lower moun-
tain, straining with the altitude but working hard to establish camps on the
steep Abruzzi Ridge. Eventually our team is ready to try for the top. Three of
us, Dan, Phil, and myself, arrive at camp 3 for our summit bid . . .

THE AIR IS HOT and still. I sit in the snow, trying to catch my breath and cool down while Dan and Phil search for any sign of our buried snow cave. Finding it means protection from the elements: the cave contains essential supplies for our stop at 7,450 meters. It took just over a month to get a few simple items to that height and to dig a cave for our shelter and cache, but now all signs of our work have been totally obliterated by the force of the recent storms. We arrived from camp 2 carrying only warm clothing and sleeping gear, and we need the stove, fuel, and food inside. Finding the snow cave is critical.

"Here it is!" After two hours of searching, Phil has located the cave entrance under more than a meter of compact snow.

The rest of the afternoon is spent expanding its capacity so the three of us can comfortably sleep in it. By sundown we finish the chore of melting snow for water and preparing dinner. Since arriving at camp 3, I have fought a disturbing feeling of nausea and I find it impossible to eat anything. I know I have to drink. The choice is simple: stay hydrated or die. I sip with difficulty at my cup of water. The thought of soup, hot chocolate, tea, or anything of substance is repulsive. It is easier not to eat, but I force myself to drink the tepid fluid.

There is plenty of room inside the snow cave, and because of the insulating qualities of snow and the heat generated by the stove and our bodies, the temperature hovers pleasantly around the freezing mark. We sleep well.

FIRST LIGHT ON JULY 6 begins a rare day on the upper slopes of K2; incredibly it is calm and clear. We can go up the broad glaciated ridge toward camp 4, the morning sun warms the air. The thermometer rises above the freezing point. Phil and Dan eat a light breakfast of snack bars and tea before we leave; I opt for water. We set off toward camp 4, moving slowly, gaining each meter of altitude with determined effort.

Our climb to camp 4 lasts seven hours. The extreme altitude reduces our pace to a crawl, and the hours pass much faster than the terrain. Our final steps to the desolate site at over 8,000 meters are agonizingly slow.

The summit of K2 dominates the shoulder where we place camp 4. We arrive there at 4:00 p.m., and I collapse to my knees and vomit the bitter green bile of an empty stomach. Painfully I gasp for breath. Thick mucous drips from my mouth. That same moment the sun is eclipsed by the massive peak above, leaving us in its icy shadow. Even in my distressed condition I notice the remarkable shift in air temperature. Instantly I start shivering.

I crawl inside the remains of a tent left by a previous expedition on K2, leaving Phil and Dan to set up our tiny bivouac tent. Five Slovenians were trapped inside this shelter – one died later of cerebral edema – and the haste with which they left is apparent. It is quite small, and I try to visualize the five men riding out a raging storm and watching their friend slip toward death. We had shared their drama in base camp, listening as broken radio transmissions described the savage weather and the steady deterioration of a team trapped by a relentless storm. The

The imposing nature of K2 is unmistakable as the mountain casts its shadow to the east over China. Five of the world's greatest peaks – Broad Peak and the four Gasherbrum peaks – catch the final rays of the day's sun on July 7, 1993. This dramatic photo was taken from camp 4 just before Dan Culver and I entered the Bottleneck on our descent. Photo: John Haigh.

four who could still walk escaped to the lower mountain during an unexpected break in the hurricane-force winds. A futile rescue effort was mounted, but their ailing partner died just below camp 4.

When I first crawled inside the tent, I felt an eerie sensation. It was as if I could envision the five men inside, as if their fear still hung in the cold air. But I shake off the mental shiver. My body is freezing, and I need to get more clothing on. There is no time for gruesome reflection.

After our tent is up, Phil crawls inside for the night and Dan joins me in the Slovenian tent to help cook and melt snow, a process I have already begun. I struggle to get warm inside my sleeping bag. The floor of the tent is uneven. I can feel the dips and bumps in the snow created by the body warmth of the five stranded climbers. I tussle with the pattern of frozen lumps under the tent, searching for a comfortable position.

Slowly, agonizingly slowly, the cold, dry snow in the pot on the stove changes into water. It is pitch-black outside and few words are spoken. I curl up in my bag and listen to my ailing body.

"Jim," Dan says suddenly, "here's some water. Can I get you anything else?"

"No." I take a couple of heavy breaths of cold air, then croak, "Thanks, Dan." Listlessly I prop myself on one elbow and accept the cup of warm water. Dan passes Phil a cup of soup through the zippered doors of the two tents, then leans back inside, closes the door, and raises a cup of hot chocolate to his cracked lips. "How are you doing, Dan?" I ask weakly.

"Tired, but okay. The weather's holding. Tomorrow's the day. We're going for the top." Dan's sentences are short and punctuated by deep breaths. "How are you doing?"

"I feel pretty feeble," I reply between small tastes of water. All I can do is sip one teaspoon of water at a time. Nausea rules my body. "Tomorrow's going to be tough."

"You'll do great. Get some sleep."

Such a statement is typical of Dan: always positive. He finishes melting the water, fills our bottles, then leaves the Slovenian tent to move in with Phil. The alarm is set for midnight, and I am alone. My utter fatigue produces two hours of restless sleep before I awake with a start at 10:30 p.m., gasping for air and crying into the night. Sudden fear dominates me. Where am I? Why can't I breathe? What makes me feel so terrible? Within seconds I remember that I am at 8,000 meters on K2. That fact answers all my questions. My heart pounds in my ears. My whole body aches. Am I going to die up here? Is this what death feels like? Such questions terrify me.

I grope for my headlamp. Light, I think, will add a sense of security to the moment. I shine it slowly around the tiny tent, staring at the few remnants left by the Slovenians: a lumpy sleeping bag, an empty fuel canister, some frozen rope. Frost is growing thickly on the inside walls. For my headache I take a four-milligram tablet of dexamethasone, a powerful medication typically used by doctors to reduce inflammation and swelling, hoping it will allow me to sleep. A small drink of ice-cold water rinses down the pill, and I lie back, knowing my chance to go to the top is only hours away.

Should I go up? Is this the start of cerebral edema? If I turn back now, I know Phil and Dan will accompany me and ruin their chance at the summit. Was I stupid to push this far? Thoughts and questions swirl around in my head before I fall into a heavy sleep.

Midnight. I light the stove and place it between our tents with a pot of snow on it. Fighting fits of grogginess, we take turns with the chore of creating water. At 2:30 a.m. I work my way out of the Slovenian tent and step into my crampons. There is a slight breeze blowing down off the summit. It is very cold. Too cold, really, but nothing less can be expected in such a place. I set off first, the hard metal points strapped to my boots biting comfortably into the wind-pressed snow. My hands and toes quickly go numb. Without bottled oxygen the chance of frostbite increases dramatically. The cold air snaps me awake. The dread of losing toes or fingers drives me forward and makes me forget about all my other misgivings. The full moon casts my shadow to the right. It is so bright that I reach up and switch off my headlamp.

I only took eight pictures above camp 4. There is so much to say about that day, and I allow each image to linger on the screen. Every slide is clear and beautiful. The colors are so vibrant: the unbelievably blue sky, Phil's bright

21

red suit, the clean white snow. It is easy to shift back to the mountain. My memories from that day are as distinct as if the events had occurred only a few hours ago.

Impulsively I share my summit mantra with the crowd. I had kept an upward pace that day by counting breaths between steps. Time on the summit day moves inexorably. It is crucial to reach the top and return to the shelter of high camp before darkness forces an exposed night outside. Such a bivouac can mean frostbite or even death. Steady upward progress is essential for safety and success. By early afternoon, at 8,400 meters, I was counting 15 breaths for every step. If I shirked, and a step took 16 or 18 breaths, my self-inflicted penalty was to take only 14 or a mere 12 deep gulps of the thin air on the following step. For 13 hours I played that game with myself, inching toward the top.

I pant 15 heavy breaths into the microphone, dragging the audience through but one of my countless summit steps. When I finish, I say, "Then I took another step." I can feel the crowd's astonishment. For a moment I know I have brought them all, breathless, to K2.

"How are your toes?" Phil asks between deep breaths as he climbs up to the ledge of rock where I have seated myself. The sun has risen above the horizon, and we are looking down on it from our perch at 8,300 meters. Its warmth floods our frigid bodies.

"I can still feel them, but they're freezing." I sit on the rocks and lift my feet toward the sun. It takes a long time for the heat of the day to reach the soles of your feet when they are busy kicking steps in the snow. "How are you guys doing?"

"Great!" is Dan's quick reply.

"I'm doin' just fine," Phil adds in his Midwestern U.S. accent. Given that we are near the top of K2, a place of potential death, it appears that we are doing "just fine."

The day is perfect. The cold, descending wind ceases with the rising of the sun, and this warm, clear day is better than we had hoped for. Phil leaves our rocky shelf and takes the lead, kicking steps up the steep snow toward The Bottleneck, the technical crux of the summit day on K2. Dan and I follow, moving up slowly, working to gain each step.

Suddenly Dan slips and starts sliding by me on the soft snow. I am startled to see the fall, but before anything can come of it Dan stops himself with his ice ax and works his way back toward the line of steps.

"Are you okay?" I yell down.

"I just slipped," he replies. "I'm on my way up." With that we all drift into our own worlds, dealing individually with the difficulty of the altitude and the increasing heat of the day. I strip off my down sweater and remove my warm hat. Looking up, I see the butt flap of Phil's down suit wide open, an obvious attempt to achieve some ventilation.

Phil leads us through The Bottleneck and onto the summit. He reaches the top just before 3:00 p.m., 12 arduous hours after leaving high camp. Alone on the summit pinnacle, Phil becomes the ninth American to accomplish the feat of climbing K2. It is his second attempt on the mountain. All his years of hard work and sacrifice have finally been rewarded.

Wisely Phil begins his descent five minutes later. At an altitude of 8,611 meters, this is no place to linger, even on such a beautiful day. He passes me on his way down. Our words are brief. "It's getting late, Jim. Do you think you should turn around now?"

I catch my breath, then say, "I feel okay. The top is pretty close. Going down should be quick."

"Do you want the radio?" he asks, always thinking of safety.

"I don't think so. We're really on our own up here, anyway." We hug, then I continue toward the top, stopping momentarily to watch as Phil descends carefully. I know he will suggest that Dan return with him to camp 4. The afternoon is passing rapidly, and Phil's concerns about getting caught in darkness are valid. Nevertheless, I am pretty certain Dan won't accept Phil's proposal, and I nod as I observe Phil continuing down alone. Dan waves at me once, then resumes the labor of his ascent.

Forty minutes later, following Phil's footprints in the wind-packed snow, I crest a tiny ridge and look over the other side. An entirely new vista appears before me –

23

mountains in every direction. Their remarkable symmetry forces me to stop and admire the scene of hundreds of peaks, some vaguely familiar to me from stories of past expeditions to the Karakoram, but I know that most are untouched, solemn and still, quiet sentinels in their frozen world. I look up and realize that only five meters away is the summit of K2.

Gripped by the moment, I forget to breathe, and the need for air hits me with a vengeance. I suck back great gulps of thin air and glance down to see if Dan is near, but he is still out of sight. I carve a small platform in the snow on the ridge, sit down, and wait for him. Our dream is to climb K2 together.

It is unusually warm for 8,600 meters, and time slips by as I wait. I absorb the wonder of the creation before me, knowing that my moments alone near the top of K2 will become a vital part of my reward. Twenty years of mountaineering, the support of my family and loved ones, and my experiences with friends in great mountain ranges around the world have led to this moment. I look down at the sea of peaks in awe.

Forty-five minutes pass before Dan comes into view. Then, shoulder to shoulder, we walk to the summit.

The shot of Dan on top of K2 illuminates the screen. The words I use to describe the image are simple: "At 4:35 in the afternoon Dan Culver and I became the first Canadians to reach the top of K2." The crowd responds with a thunderous ovation, and I am overcome with pride. Their reaction is spontaneous, a reward for an achievement. It takes a long minute or two before the tribute ends. Strangely I don't feel embarrassed, only strengthened by their support.

With the press of a button, the image of Dan on the summit gradually disappears and the screen fades to black. The slides are finished, but the tale is far from over. The auditorium darkens, save for a small glow on the podium where I stand. It is time to tell the most difficult part of the story.

Only a handful of people have ever reached the top of K2. It isn't until that moment, when we stand on the summit, that we realize such an achievement is

25

The sweeping view to the east from near the summit on K2. The Godwin-Austen Glacier cuts through the heart of the Karakoram Range where it meets with the Baltoro Glacier at Concordia.

possible for us. I have already been on top for more than an hour, and to linger any longer would be a grave mistake; the few remaining hours of daylight are precious, and movement at over 8,600 meters is desperately slow. We leave K2's pinnacle and focus on the descent.

It is often trickier to go down a mountain than it is to go up one, especially one like K2. Dan and I remind each other to be careful, then set off slowly. We move together, yet we both know that we are each very much on our own. Climbing a mountain like K2 is a team effort, but above 8,000 meters the equation changes. As a team, we had chosen to climb without a rope for speed and safety, all of us aware of the risks and the benefits.

The descent from the top is a lonely time. I concentrate on every step, focusing only on the moment. My crampons bite securely into the hard snow below The Bottleneck; I am happy to be past that crux. I glance over my shoulder and see Dan enter the top of the steep section 100 meters above me. My own safety requires concentration on the task at hand, and I immediately return to my steps.

Suddenly, like the shattering of glass, a noise breaks my concentration. I spin and see Dan cartwheeling past me. His blond hair stands out in the chaos of his tumbling body and allows me to imagine his terror as he falls out of sight down the South Face. He is moving so quickly that it seems as if nothing will slow him down.

Nothing . . .

I will never know for certain what happened to Dan that afternoon. Perhaps he was hit by a piece of falling ice, or maybe he caught his crampon in the snow. When I reach this part in my story, the audience is completely silent. I am left in the dark with no slides to support me, and I fight unsuccessfully to suppress the grief surging up from deep within.

Everyone waits patiently. They understand. As I relive the moment – the emotions and the fear – I am carried along by the energy and silent support of everyone gathered here. This time I am not alone as I shed the tears needed to grapple with the death of my friend, Dan Culver.

In an unfamiliar way, I have begun to climb another mountain.

26

Our team was joined by dozens of climbers from base camp to pay a tribute to Dan at the Gilkey Memorial. This cairn was erected in 1953 by a group of Americans in remembrance of their friend and partner, Art Gilkey, who died that year on the mountain.

27

Sparring with the Devil's Thumb
On the Edge in the Wilds of Alaska

THE SNOW WAS PERFECT for the ascent. Both ice tools penetrated smoothly and securely; my crampons bit the avalanche-swept surface with confidence. Repetition of the climbing action began to nudge me into a trance. Place one tool – test. Place the second tool – test. Alternate up with each foot, making sure the crampon's metal front points are fixed in the ice. Then do it all over again. It seemed strange that in the steep, narrow gully between the Cat's Ears Spire and the Devil's Thumb I might be slipping into a daydream. There are few places on the planet more severe and uncharitable. These giant granite towers rise from a sea of ice on the remote border between British Columbia and Alaska where the weather is invariably savage. The temperament of the Devil's Thumb is wild, cold, and merciless: snow, rock, ice, wind, and clouds.

But my world was limited to the range of my headlamp, and headlamps have a hypnotic effect after a while. I could see only two meters up or down. The vertical rock walls that enclosed the gully were close enough that, if I turned my head to either side, the gray granite would furnish a dull reflection. The intense feeling of enclosure warned me to concentrate on the snow and ice in front of me.

I could hear my teammates below: Michael Down, a longtime friend, explorer, and student of the mountains who had fashioned dozens of first ascents up sheer faces and buttresses on remote peaks in western North America; and Alastair Foreman, a talented technical climber and my reliable partner on many mountain adventures. Both were methodically following the series of marks my ice tools and crampons had left in the snow. It was still early in the day, and I was thankful that

29

The North Face of the Devil's Thumb from the Stikine Icecap. The narrow summit provides an exact point of reference on the border of British Columbia and southeastern Alaska.

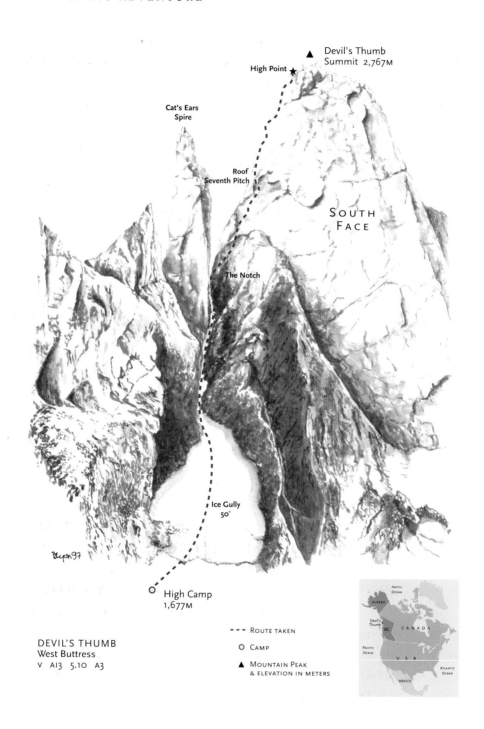

▲ Devil's Thumb
Summit 2,767M

High Point ★

Cat's Ears
Spire

Roof
Seventh Pitch

SOUTH
FACE

The Notch

Ice Gully
50°

Btypn97

○ High Camp
1,677M

DEVIL'S THUMB
West Buttress
V AI3 5.10 A3

- - - ROUTE TAKEN

○ CAMP

▲ MOUNTAIN PEAK
& ELEVATION IN METERS

ARCTIC
OCEAN

ALASKA

Devil's
Thumb
BC

CANADA

PACIFIC
OCEAN

U.S.A.

ATLANTIC
OCEAN

MEXICO

dawn would soon be coming. The trance made climbing easier.

We reached the top of the 60-degree couloir at 5:30 a.m., our calves aching from the effort. We were almost two hours earlier than our second attempt on the route, and a full five hours faster than our first try a week earlier. Time would have to be our ally if we were going to reach the summit this time; it was to be our final bid for the top. The sky had lost its stars to the dull light of the coming day.

We anchored to the rock of the Devil's Thumb at the top of the gully in an exposed notch between our objective and the Cat's Ears Spire. It was a frightening place. Both peaks towered above; in the cold shadows it seemed as if the mountain had us completely enclosed. A quick look down the other side of the notch left me reeling with a sense of vertigo. The ice-covered rock of the north face plummeted 1,200 meters into the Witches Cauldron, a rare glacial feature where all of the surrounding rivers of ice meet one another in a stagnant sinkhole. Our only options out of the dark cleft into which we had climbed were back down the gully or up the Thumb in search of the sunrise and the summit.

"That was fast," Alastair said, breaking our momentary silence. "We're making great time and the sun's not even up. Let's go boys!"

We ascended the fixed ropes, lines we had left in place from our previous efforts, and that put us 70 meters up from the notch in under two hours. Then, resting on the only big ledge on the route, one meter wide by two meters long, we prepared ourselves for the climb ahead. It was still bitterly cold, but we knew that eventually the sun would heat up our day. In anticipation of the steep and technical granite above, we laced on our slipperlike rock shoes with stiff, frigid fingers. Meanwhile we carefully stored our precious double boots that we had worn on the ice and snow of the couloir, ready to be picked up on the descent later that day. Michael took the first lead while Alastair and I shivered and waited.

An hour later the still morning was broken by a cry from above – "Secure!"

Michael's effort was over. His shout was the standard choice from the climber's vocabulary, and Alastair and I knew immediately what was happening. He had built an anchor at the top of the pitch, and it was now time for Alastair and me to move up. I went first, sliding my mechanical ascenders – or jumars – up the rope, earning a mere 30 centimeters with each manipulation. Jumaring is strenuous work, but I was grateful for the heat generated by the effort that wintry morning, and I was warm by the time I reached Michael's perch, a ledge big enough for only three of our four feet. We exchanged gear and I was away. It was my task to lead the next pitch, and efficient use of time was critical if we wanted to reach the top.

IT WAS OUR THIRD attempt in two weeks at climbing the West Buttress of the Devil's Thumb, and this was my second expedition to the mountain. Ten years earlier my brother Kevin and I had come here but had been stymied by lack of experience and the dreadful weather that dominates this part of North America.

The British Columbia-Alaska border is a dramatic alpine wilderness separating the temperate rainforest of southeastern Alaska from the much drier interior plateau on the Canadian side. Relentless glaciers carve their way to the ocean, originating on the high divide of the Coast Mountains where massive icefields act as glacial spawning grounds. Their blue icebergs floating in the steep-walled fjords provide an arresting foreground for the green hemlock and cedar forests. The striking beauty of coastal Alaska draws tens of thousands of tourists every year, most on luxury cruise ships. Those who travel into the vast wilderness on foot, by sail, or in kayaks are scarce.

To the west lies the Gulf of Alaska, a brooding, tempestuous sea that generates almost all of the poor weather that buffets the Pacific coast of North America. Low-pressure systems spawned in the gulf produce hundreds of storms every year, ranging from mild spring showers to hurricane-force gales bearing massive quantities of precipitation. The amount of rain that falls on southeastern Alaska is staggering: the wettest places in the region drown in more than six meters every year. The weather in its remote peaks and valleys reflects these statistics.

Although only 800 kilometers long, southeastern Alaska contains more than 20,000 kilometers of shoreline and over 1,000 islands. By contrast, there are fewer than 300 kilometers of year-round highway. Locals move by plane or by boat, and fishing and logging are the main elements of the economy.

We had arrived by air from Seattle, landing in Petersburg, Alaska, on May 22, 1990, a day of steel-gray skies and mist clinging to the ridges. The granite tower of the Devil's Thumb dominates the view from Petersburg, but that day it was buried

32

My brother Kevin approaches the Devil's Thumb across the Stikine Icecap in the summer of 1981. We traveled to the mountain by kayaking down the Stikine River, then hiked up the Flood Glacier but were unsuccessful in our attempt on the mountain. Ten years later I returned to try the peak again.

deep in the clouds. We carried our gear across the runway to the Temsco Helicopters hangar and introduced ourselves. We were told the pilot was out flying but would be back in a couple of hours. Not caring to simply wait around, we took a taxi into town to explore and enjoy our last meal in civilization for the next 24 days.

Guarding the entrance to Wrangell Narrows, Petersburg is a classic Alaskan fishing town located on the northern tip of Mitkof Island. Originally the site was chosen for its proximity to tidal glaciers, which provided a ready supply of ice for fish processing. Today the main street of the town that sprang up around the plant etches a line following the contour of a protected harbor, while its houses find shelter on the forested hillside above. All activity revolves around the water. There are hundreds of boats of all shapes and sizes – commercial seiners to recreational jet boats – moored along the dozens of docks and floats. Canneries, tackle shops, gas barges, and shipyards complete the picture of a fishing town. Even after a rainfall the air offers the sharp odor of fish. The commercial fishing industry, its set-

The Devil's Thumb dominates the horizon above the Alaskan fishing village of Petersburg. Photo: Tom Ellison.

backs and its successes, generates the headlines in the local newspaper and dominates conversations in the pubs and restaurants. There are virtually no suits and
ties on the streets of Petersburg; the garb is mostly rubber boots, rain gear, and oil-
stained baseball caps. The lifestyle of coastal Alaska is in clear evidence. Logging
and forestry are important industries, but the town lives and breathes fishing.

By the time we returned to the hangar, our pilot, Doc, had come back from his
previous flight and it was our turn to pack up the helicopter and go. Doc was a
youthful 40-something pilot who had done his training in Vietnam. A big man with
a bushy black mustache and a crew cut, he could have easily been an intimidating presence, but his quick smile and friendly manner softened any severe first
impression. While we loaded up the tiny Hughes 500 helicopter, he pointed out
his refrigerator in the hangar and told us to help ourselves to moose steaks and
beer when we returned from our trip.

Alastair and I were on the first flight, and we landed at our base camp at 600
meters on the Witches Cauldron Glacier. We didn't get the aerial views of the
Devil's Thumb we had hoped for; in fact, as a result of limited visibility and a light
drizzle, we flew the entire way only 30 meters above the ground. Doc kept the
Hughes fired up while we unloaded gear, then he lifted, turned, and was gone
down the glacier into the darkening afternoon to pick up Michael.

By the time Doc and Michael returned, the light rain had increased to a steady
downpour. Before the distinct beat of the disappearing helicopter faded completely, we began to work in organized desperation to set up tents in order to keep
our mountain of gear as dry as possible. We had food for a little more than three
weeks and all the rock- and ice-climbing equipment needed to reach our goal –
the summit of the Devil's Thumb.

By noon the following day the rain and clouds had changed to clear skies and
sunshine, a transformation typical of the area's unpredictable weather patterns,
and we took advantage of the brightness to get out and explore. In every direction
we could see sheer granite walls, tumbling glacial icefalls, and jagged peaks. But
it was the remoteness of our situation that eclipsed even the stunning beauty: we
were days of travel from the ocean, there was no human settlement within at least
two weeks' walk of our camp, and we knew of no other climbers active in the

range. Our scheduled pickup at the head of the fjord was 24 days away.

The next day the unsettled weather returned and we spent an entire week waiting for conditions to improve. One day was spent shuffling our gear up the glacier to the south side of the mountain, but mostly we stayed inside the tent listening to the rain on the fly. Finally, on May 30, bound for the summit, we left base camp at 2:30 a.m. under starry skies.

It was our second time through the icefall that guards the approach to the mountain, and familiarity with the lower route made our predawn trip easier. We began climbing the ice gully between the Cat's Ears Spire and the Thumb just after 7:00 a.m. It was long, steep, and icy.

Michael panted. "This is taking longer than we thought."

I agreed with a nod, but Alastair offered a touch of optimism. "We'll make it."

There wasn't much more conversation. Each of us drifted back into our own thoughts and battled the upward slope of the gully.

We climbed two rope lengths, or pitches, of rock from the top of the gully beginning from the narrow notch between the two granite spires, but by early afternoon clouds were racing across the icecap to the west and soon engulfed the mountain in mist and falling snow. Retreating, we left two ropes in place to facilitate a return to our high point, knowing we still had plenty of time to come back and try again. The knowledge we had gained about the route would make subsequent attempts more efficient.

Escaping down the gully in the relative warmth of midday proved to be a nasty experience. The Cat's Ears Spire, still coated in its winter sheath of rime, was shedding huge chunks of ice. The sound these made as they fell, unhindered for hundreds of meters off the vertical-to-overhanging rock, was a loud, piercing whistle. Then there would be an abrupt end to this unnerving sound when the ice bombs thudded into the gully, exploding violently and sending nuggets of ice in all directions like popcorn in a pot.

Our choices weren't too appealing: trust our luck and start down the gully, or wait in the exposed, windy notch for the evening's cooler temperatures. As we discussed our options, an enormous mass of ice crashed into the gully just below where we stood. The mountain seemed to shake with the impact; we decided to wait.

Michael aid-climbs on the cold granite of the Devil's Thumb.

Two hours later the barrage from the Cat's Ears grew silent. Our bodies cold and stiff, we slid down our ropes and returned to base camp. At 10:00 p.m. we staggered up to our tent, tired and hungry. Dinner was a simple meal of soup, crackers, and cheese. Sleep came easily.

Round one to the Devil's Thumb.

Our next attempt began three days later at 2:30 a.m. It was June 2, Michael's birthday. Knowing what to expect from the terrain, we moved quickly up the ice gully, the ropes that had been left in place from the previous attempt speeding us to our former high point. We launched ourselves up the unknown buttress, hoping to reach the summit by late afternoon. However, the rock was coated in fresh snow from the two-day storm between our attempts, frustrating our efforts to move quickly. The clock outpaced the speed of our ascent. After eight hours of climbing, we were only six pitches up the route and there were still four or five to go. Again the weather was deteriorating. We debated the advantage of a cold night on a ledge higher on the route – a worthy gamble had there been clear skies – but with the howling wind and a light snow falling it was obvious that descent was our only option.

We retreated past the familiar features, rappelling to the notch and down the gully to the glacier. Nineteen hours after starting up, we were safely back in our tent.

Round two to the Devil's Thumb.

FIVE DAYS LATER I found myself leading out from Michael's belay stance and quickly realized how cold the rock was. The heat I had retained from jumaring was promptly expended, and my fingers and toes rapidly turned into insensitive stumps. Fortunately the difficult climbing on my pitch was mostly at the start and, despite the sting of cold digits, I managed to stretch the rope to the small alcove I had climbed to on our second attempt. Once there, I sat down and warmed my hands. My knowledge of the pitch from our last attempt provided a mental advantage and helped me move forward with confidence despite the cold. I set an anchor and yelled down to Michael that I was secure and he could begin climbing. That same instant the morning sun came around the corner of the huge south

39

Michael searching for the route on the third pitch of the West Buttress. To the west, peaks rise from the mass of the Stikine Icecap.

buttress of the Devil's Thumb and flooded my little perch with warmth and light. I basked in the heat, absorbing the radiant energy like a sponge. It was 9:45 a.m.

Michael led through in the sunshine and scrambled efficiently up the easier rock above. Alastair came up to my perch and followed Michael's lead, leaving me to take up the final position on our rope. We were taking turns leading in order to share the workload and conserve energy for what was certain to be a very long day. I soaked up as much heat as possible before I departed my alcove for Alastair and Michael's station above. The wind was beginning to blow, and I hoped that it was a result of the day heating up rather than yet another system of poor weather streaming in from the west.

By the time I had followed on jumars to the top of our fifth pitch, Alastair was already finishing his lead. It was an exposed and technical portion of our route with scant protection against a fall. Alastair managed it in businesslike fashion; after only 20 minutes, the anchor was set.

"Great lead, Alastair!" I yelled encouragingly up to him. Then I turned to Michael. "We're really moving. I just hope this weather holds."

"It looks to me like it's changing for the worse," he said, "but maybe not. This is our last chance." He prepared to follow Alastair's lead, then added, "Anyway, I'll go for the roof and we'll just have to keep an eye on those clouds. See you up there." And he was off, concentrating on the delicate movements needed to climb the pitch.

Michael had the most experience aid-climbing, a painstaking technique whereby a climber stands on gear placements to move up, unlike free-climbing, where a climber ascends by connecting holds on the rock using only feet and hands. Equipment in free-climbing is placed as a fail-safe in case of a fall.

Michael shot past Alastair to grapple with the roof above. From our previous high point, we knew that this part of the route would require crafty equipment placement to enable us to get past the almost featureless overhangs. Michael's background in such situations made him our best choice to manage the problem.

By the time I arrived at Alastair's belay site, Michael was out to the edge of the roof. As I watched him deal with the overhang, what struck me was the speed with which the misty clouds blew by his position. As he surmounted the roof and tried to explore new vertical ground past the ceiling, winds in excess of 50 kilometers per hour ripped across the face.

Obviously a change in the weather was coming. Thick, low clouds, which at 9:00 a.m. were 40 kilometers to the west and covered only the ocean, now engulfed the peaks to the southwest of the Devil's Thumb. We still had mostly blue skies above, but mist was beginning to swirl and the shift to a squall seemed certain.

Michael tried desperately to aid-climb his way to easier ground, but a single move eluded him. No matter what gear combinations he tried, none would hold his weight. "I can't get anything in here!" he screamed back to us into the wind. "Everything just pops out."

His options were to put in an expansion bolt – a tedious and time-consuming process – retreat, or attempt to climb past the thin section without the aid of gear. "My hands are freezing!" he yelled back to us over the lashing wind. "But I'm going to go for it. Watch the rope. I may fall."

Stepping from the slings he was using as an aid, Michael committed to the move. "I got it!" he shouted jubilantly. He seemed to be talking to himself as much

Alastair belays and watches as Michael works in gusting wind to climb over the roof at mid-height on the first ascent of the West Buttress of the Devil's Thumb.

as letting us know how it was. Then he yelled back down, "The move's okay! I'll go up and set a belay." As he disappeared, Alastair and I waited while the rope that connected us to our friend above slowly payed out with each upward move he made. We huddled in the hanging stance, shifting our positions occasionally to change the uncomfortable pressure of our harnesses from one sore spot to another.

Alastair followed on jumars once Michael had given the familiar cry of "Secure!" The ropes were solidly attached to the rock at the top of his lead. The weather had now decisively changed and was deteriorating. Our day had shifted from a hard rock climb on a sunny day to a struggle for the top in an approaching storm.

The next pitch looked challenging, and Alastair was ahead dealing with the most difficult moves by the time I caught up to Michael on the small ledge he had reached after climbing through the roof. "Great lead back there, Michael," I said admiringly, puffing. "It looked pretty thin."

Michael concentrated on Alastair's lead, attentive to the rope. "What do you think about the weather?" he asked without letting his eyes drift from his immediate responsibility – our partner ahead on the rock.

"Looks like it's changing for sure. Maybe it'll hold off snowing for a while, though," I said, more hopeful than confident.

As we spoke, I took the opportunity to put on my shell clothing. The wind was cold and it was my turn to lead as soon as Alastair was done. That fate came minutes later as he anchored himself and I followed on a belay from above. By the time I reached the ledge at the end of his difficult pitch, it had started to snow lightly. Alastair was hunched inside a shallow corner, hiding from the wind. Looking ahead to the next section of rock, I grabbed the gear from him and said, "This weather's getting bad. What do you think?"

"It's our last chance for this trip," he replied, "and we're nearly there. Let's wait and see what Michael thinks."

I moved slowly left from the belay stance and waited on the nearby ledge. "Okay. I'll wait until Michael arrives. We can decide then. I just don't want to get cold waiting."

Michael had begun to follow Alastair's lead on ascenders. A rope length below, in the mist and drifting snow, his jumars were slipping on the icy rope. I could hear him cursing uncharacteristically. Down and to my right, Alastair had curled himself up with his back to the wind. He appeared mindful of the belay despite his increasing discomfort.

Up or down? That question was on all our minds. Safety is an easy excuse for retreat, and we had already used it twice in the past two weeks. On both of those occasions it had been the right decision. Our weather luck continued to be terrible. This was our last chance. We were out of time. The mountain would wait for our next trip, but I asked myself whether I would ever again find myself so close to this summit.

I changed my mind and decided to climb on before Michael reached Alastair for a group discussion. "I'm going up, Alastair!" I yelled into the wind. "If Michael wants to go back when he gets here, I'll rappel down and we can get out of here. But if we're going for it, I'll be up there already." "Go for it, Jimmy, but be careful," Alastair said, continuing his cheerleading as I moved up the rock in front of me. Although the top was near, it was more important than ever to focus on the task at hand. I set out on the face, concentrating, one move at a time.

Despite the falling snow, the climbing was great: there were flakes and edges to gain purchase and lots of small cracks in which to place chocks and cams for protection against the possibility of a fall. The poor weather was the only drawback; on a warm, sunny day I knew the cracks and corners of the West Buttress of the Devil's Thumb would provide for a classic outing. But my fingers were freezing, and the moves on that pitch were much too hard to allow the luxury of wearing mitts or gloves.

I reached a belay stance only a rope length below the summit block, tied myself to the anchor, and screamed into the storm, "Secure! Jumar when ready." Given the wind and the distance to my partners, I kept communication simple. There was no time for errors or wasteful actions. Michael followed on jumars up the snow-covered line, and I studied the steep corner above. I was getting cold and decided that I wanted the next lead so I could warm up. The top was so close. The next lead was supposed to be Michael's, and I wondered how I could ask for

Michael jumars iced ropes on the Devil's Thumb.

it without insulting him. I thought of Alastair, and I knew he must be feeling miserable after crouching on that small ledge for more than an hour. The wind and snow intensified.

Michael struggled to the belay, panting with the effort. His jumars had slipped badly on the rope. His first words to me were: "Do you mind taking the next lead?"

There was no discussion. In an instant I was on my way up the final corner. It was the most difficult pitch of the climb. The cold crack in the back of the corner was slightly overhanging and roughly the width of my fist. The pure physical strain of the climbing was indisputable. As I climbed, I shuffled our largest camming unit up the crack with me, using it for both protection and rests. Soon the rope dangled 20 meters down the snow-covered rock to Michael, with only two pieces of gear between us. But when I pulled over the top, I found a solid ledge where I could build a good anchor.

Less than 30 meters above was the summit. I tied off the line and yelled down for Michael to jumar. Then I waited, pushing myself into the wall, trying to hide from the weather to preserve some of my newly earned warmth. Snow piled up at my feet, and within 20 minutes 10 centimeters of wind-driven powder surrounded my thin rock shoes.

Michael arrived and it took us little time to reach a decision. We would have to be satisfied that we had climbed a new route on this wild and challenging mountain. There would be no summit. The low-angled, blocky terrain above was a perfect spot for rappel ropes to get caught. Another hour or two near the exposed summit might get us into real trouble. It was 6:00 p.m. We didn't want to lose what control we had left. "We're coming down!" I screamed to Alastair.

The storm continued and the wind drove snow into every crack and corner. The Cat's Ears Spire, its dark, jagged rock dramatically coated with fresh white snow, jutted through the swirling clouds below as Michael leaned back on the iced-up ropes. He took a customary last glance at the anchor, mumbled something to himself, then descended into the murk. The three of us continued down the Devil's Thumb, rappelling into the fading light of day.

Then came the night. Standing on a ledge that seemed to grow smaller as the sky darkened, we constantly checked and rechecked our knots, slings, and gear

Mist and cloud from yet another Pacific storm swirl around the South Face of the Devil's Thumb and force retreat from the mountain.

placements. There were no bivouac spots. As a result of the moisture in the storm, the smooth rock was coated in a thin veneer of ice – verglas, the climber's dread. We had committed to the route with little extra clothing. Scantily clad in rock shoes, our toes froze; warm fingers were a thing of the past. Waiting for the dawn in the rising wind and driving snow on a small perch high on the Devil's Thumb might have been worse than uncomfortable. We continued our descent into the darkness.

Michael rappelled down. All that Alastair and I could see at the end of the rope was the beam of our team's single headlamp on Michael's helmet. Below him was the huge unclimbed northwest face of the Thumb; we knew it was 1,500 meters to the Witches Cauldron. Then, finally, we heard the welcome sound of "Off rappel!" Michael had built another anchor and we could slide down when ready. His shout energized us on our dark, silent ledge.

Now we continually reminded ourselves not to be hasty and make mistakes. After double-checking his gear in the darkness, Alastair rappelled out of sight. His departure left me temporarily alone, anchored to the mountain by bits of rope and a couple of pitons driven into the rock. The snow continued to blow across the face of the mountain, and I huddled to keep warm. Had the sky been clear I could have seen the distant lights of Petersburg. They might have provided a sense of comfort.

I rappelled to where Michael and Alastair stood nestled in the darkness. While I organized the rack of gear and put on the headlamp, Alastair pulled the ropes and Michael worked them through the new anchor. It was my turn to go first. Down I went, the headlamp beam searching anxiously for the next station. It was just past midnight and we were halfway down the Devil's Thumb.

Each rappel passed slowly as we struggled with anchors and frozen ropes. We encouraged and sought encouragement from one another, fighting fear with jokes and carefully examining every move we made.

When we reached the big ledge where we had stashed our double boots 18 hours earlier, it was a joy to pull on dry socks, cold boot liners, and outside shells. Our feet gradually warmed and lent a new sense of security to a situation that teetered on the edge of control.

Two more rope lengths down would lead us to the top of the ice gully, but we still had a long way to go. The notch was only two meters wide at the top and it was crucial that we hit the south side. That would lead us to our ascent route, the gully that plunged 500 meters through vertical rock to the glacier below. If we missed the notch and ended up on the northwest face, the wrong side of the mountain, it would be a staggering 1,200 meters to the Witches Cauldron. We would run out of anchor material long before reaching the bottom of that monster. Overshooting the notch wasn't an option. I set off from the ledge in the inky blackness toward our target.

In the dark I unintentionally passed an old anchor we had used on the previous two descents. Snow and ice covered everything. Alastair and Michael must have wondered what was taking so long.

I was scared. I dangled at the end of the rope, skidding around on the verglas-covered rock, all the while searching with the tiny beam of my headlamp for a crack – anything to pound some iron into. The darkness and rushing wind heightened my anxiety. I struggled for control of my fear and continued the quest for an anchor site.

Finally I found a 60-centimeter seam in the icy black rock. It was less than a centimeter wide, but it was deep, so I smashed two pitons into it until I knew they could take no more punishment. There was no ledge for my feet, and after tying the two pieces together, I attached myself and eased my weight onto the anchor. I knew it was solid, but my mind was having trouble accepting that logic.

"Off rappel!" I screamed into the night. The sound disappeared into the wind. "Off rappel!" I yelled again between gusts. Then the ropes moved and I knew that my cries had been heard. I curled up into a ball and hung off the anchor, hiding, waiting for my partners to come and join me in the middle of nowhere.

With three of us on the anchor it was difficult to move without imagining what might happen if the thing gave way. There was no good reason to contemplate such thoughts, but it was impossible not to. We lowered the ropes off the anchor, knowing that the notch and the ice gully we had climbed so many hours ago were somewhere below. I left the station first, fighting the iced-up ropes, confident that my next anchor would be in the gully.

48

A sense of relief swept over me when I touched down on the snow and ice of the gully. Despite the darkness, we now had a confined and clear route to follow. We continued down, anxious to be off the mountain.

Waiting for daylight on a cold bivouac in the mountains is an agonizing process. It always comes too slowly. We had spent the entire night descending and were so engaged that when the gray light of dawn made our headlamp unnecessary it came as a pleasant surprise. It felt grand just to see the walls of rock and ice that surrounded us. Although intimidating, the terrain was familiar and the glow of dawn helped banish the goblins of apprehension from our heads.

We reached our camp at 7:00 a.m. on June 8, 27 hours after starting out. The descent had required 17 rappels, many during the darkest hours of night. We were tired and battered, but happy, finally, to relax. We collapsed into the tent, lethargic and indifferent to the needs of our bodies.

Lying on my sleeping bag, still in my harness, I reflected on our effort. The fact that we didn't reach the summit left me with an empty feeling. I knew we had essentially finished the route – it would have only been a scramble to the top – and that the only smart and safe decision was to turn back when we did. Yet, despite all my rationalizing, being driven from the mountain when the summit was so close still bothered me. I knew my feelings of regret were part of something I had learned, part of the competitive, achievement-oriented drive that our society had bred into me. I battled those proud emotions with the knowledge that the route was classic and that we had climbed it in good style in the company of one another. The summit would certainly have added to the already high quality of our experience, but perhaps it would have come at the expense of safety. And these are games of survival, not unjustified heroics.

We gave it a good fight and learned from our efforts, but the final round went, as before, to the Devil's Thumb.

Weathering the Unknown
Ski Mountaineering in the Hidden Himalayas

"It will be no problem, sir," Amar said with quiet confidence.

Our chief porter, or *sirdar*, was referring to the size and weight of the porters' loads and their ability to manage them. On that sunny spring morning in March 1995, Amar's comment prompted my thoughts to wander from the porters' loads to the journey we were proposing. Experience had taught me that our ski tour into the poorly mapped wilderness of India's Himalayas, through high passes and across Alaskan-sized glaciers, could be expected to produce problems enough.

My partner Sue Oakey and I had hauled our skis, boots, and related equipment through several airports around the world – places where baggage handlers, check-in clerks, and taxi drivers had likely never seen skis. For two months we had manhandled the awkward, two-meter package through the Third World disorder of equatorial Africa to the sizzling hot lowlands of the Indian subcontinent and from there to the Himalayan foothills. Despite all of the frustration, we would soon be gliding over pristine, untracked snow on the high mountains surrounding the town of Manali.

We had left New Delhi on March 9, traveling north by bus on a major highway until it joined a narrow road heading toward the foothills. It followed a course along lush valley bottoms before spiraling up from the rivers on an improbable track etched into the side of the mountains to gain the height needed to reach the distant alpine villages. In the days before independence in 1947, wealthy British colonials took this route each summer to escape the stifling heat of the Indian plains. The road appeared not to have been paved for some years, perhaps since

51

Sue Oakey ascends an unnamed glacier, the source of the
Manalsu Nala, en route to Hanuman
Tibba near Manali, India.

Lord Mountbatten had signed the orders for independence. Potholes, blind corners, and washed-out sections made a 400-kilometer journey to Manali last for 18
bumpy hours.

We slept very little on the lurching, rattling bus, and the long night gave me
time to reflect on the circumstances that had led Sue and me to this mountainous area of India. With only the vaguest of plans for a spring ski tour – developed
over the telephone several months earlier – we planned a stop in India on our
round-the-world trip. There we expected to meet a longtime friend, Rob Orvig, a
mountain guide from Canada who had been spending his winter guiding helicopter skiing in Manali. Together we hoped to explore one of the lesser known and
remote areas of the Himalayas.

As we stepped off the bus into the chilly morning air, we were besieged by the
usual mob of idle rickshaw and taxi drivers in search of business. Our few days in
India hadn't toughened us yet against their aggressiveness, but after a sleepless night
on a noisy bus we were too tired to be pleasant. Gruffly brushing aside their

Sue walks through the streets of Manali in search of a hotel to catch a shower and rest in a
bed after several days of backcountry skiing in the nearby mountains.

advances, we hoisted our packs and slung our skis over our shoulders. For an instant, doubt entered our minds: why had we come thousands of kilometers from home to ski in a place we knew so little about? Fatigue dulled our sense of adventure.

"We're like a couple of pack mules," Sue said, and we shared a tired laugh. "Look at all the stuff we're lugging!"

"There's no point in hanging out here," I said wearily. "Let's go try to find Rob." And we set off through the bustling streets of Manali in search of our only contact point in town, the office of Himalayan Journeys.

We found the office quickly and were given a very friendly reception along with a note from Rob. Before we could even read it our loads were gently lifted from our backs, chairs were brought out of the back room, and *chai*, a sweet, milky tea, was ordered from a stall down the street. Sue and I were then politely introduced to Iqubal and Indra, owners of the company, their friendly office staff, and the head guide, Amar.

Our chai arrived and we relaxed in the company of new friends, free from the pressures of the persistent hustlers on the street. Rob's hastily penned message was dated March 8 and gave us only a few basic details. The heli-skiing season was over, and he had taken advantage of a departing helicopter to hitch a ride to another range of mountains for a hut-based ski tour with some friends. He would be back on March 18 and was still keen to join us on a ski adventure at that time.

This delay suited Sue and me very well. We needed time to get acclimatized to the altitude and the cold, and to develop the level of fitness that would be essential for an extended ski tour in the Himalayas. The plan was set: we would do several shorter trips ourselves, then join Rob for a longer journey on March 20.

The next 10 days were dedicated to skiing in the mountains near Manali. The alpine terrain was reminiscent of the Selkirk Mountains back home in Canada, complete with big trees, wide-open bowls, and a background of craggy summits. We enjoyed some fine tours in several different areas.

Another benefit to us of this additional time was the opportunity to become gradually familiar with the customs of the friendly people of the Kullu Valley, and it didn't take long before we felt at home among the many cultures represented in this small mountain town – the native Indians, Nepalese immigrants, and a small presence of Tibetan refugees who had come there to escape oppression following the Chinese invasion of Tibet in 1959. Our favorite eating place in Manali became a small Tibetan-run restaurant on the main street. Whenever we stepped inside to escape the frosty spring air, the welcome heat of the glowing woodstove in the middle of the room warmed us. The traditional food was served with an appreciative smile, and each visit was a highlight of our day.

India is a country of extremes. It is a vast landmass rising from the tropical Indian Ocean and extending more than 3,000 kilometers north to the Himalayan Mountains, the highest peaks on Earth. The climate, although generally warm and enjoyable, can be cruel: temperatures in the summer months in the southern and central parts of the country are unbearably hot, while winter in the mountain villages in the Himalayas and the northern districts of Kashmir and Ladakh can be desperately cold. Annual monsoon rains, the lifeblood of many portions of the country, regularly flood entire cities. More than 900 million people are crammed inside India's borders, and the population is exploding. In a few years India will surpass China as the world's most populated country.

While there is incredible historic wealth in India, hundreds of millions of people live at levels of hopeless poverty. The country's intriguing history traces an ancient culture in which religion has always played an important role in the everyday life of the people. Many of the country's special customs are derived from religious traditions that have developed through the ages, yet the unresolved conflict between Hindu and Muslim is one of modern India's most perplexing dilemmas. Our journey to these mountain regions was to be as much a cultural experience as a skiing adventure.

By the time Rob returned to Manali, Sue and I were physically and mentally ready for our adventure of exploration deeper into the mountains and the little-known peaks and valleys rising to the north. We met at our usual restaurant for lunch. Over bowls of sweet and sour soup and plates of steamed vegetable *momos*, a traditional Tibetan dish, the route was set.

Our goal was to do a traverse through the solitary valleys to the west of town. The route would start in Manali and come out of the mountains 50 kilometers to the north by way of the Beas Kund, a steep valley and dramatic mountain cathedral of

54

sheer alpine walls and lofty summits; local inquiries convinced us that no one had ever skied through the area. In total, we would travel for seven or eight days, ending our trip in the tiny village of Solang. Along the way we hoped to climb Hanuman Tibba: rising to more than 5,900 meters, it was one of the highest peaks on the traverse.

We left Manali the following morning – the first day of spring – at 8:00 a.m. Amar had hired three Nepalese porters to carry our packs for the first two days up the trail. We had brought eight days' supply of food, rope, and equipment for glacier travel, as well as plenty of warm clothing needed for winter camping at 5,000 meters in the Himalayas. To these loads we added our skis and bulky ski-touring boots. With our ski gear attached to the packs, the normal porter-sized loads became awkward, cumbersome burdens. Rob, Sue, and I flipped our day packs over our shoulders and, feeling a bit guilty, followed Amar and our porters through the streets of Manali.

The warm morning sun greeted our company of seven as we marched up the narrow lanes of the old village. The sweet scent of wood smoke hung in the air, and the locals were already busy with their daily chores: fetching water in brass canisters, scrubbing clothes on flat rocks by the area's solitary water pipe, rolling and cooking chapatis over glowing coals, chopping wood, weaving, and generally living as they have for centuries. The scene was right out of a storybook: children, perhaps lacking the pride and inhibitions of their elders, pestered us for candies or possibly a pen for school; a mother breast-fed her infant child in the sun; old men sat together, quietly exchanging small talk at the start of another day; two young women braided each other's hair, giggling and watching curiously as we passed by.

Our expedition was a striking contrast to their lives. Whenever we had chatted with the locals about our plans to ski from Manali to Solang via Hanuman Tibba and the Beas Kund, we were flatly told it wasn't possible. And why would anyone want to do it, anyway? This was a difficult question to answer at any time, but impossible to explain in broken English to people who spend the majority of their lives simply surviving. Our pursuit of recreation and adventure, what made us feel alive – to ski through and explore the high-mountain country – was beyond their means.

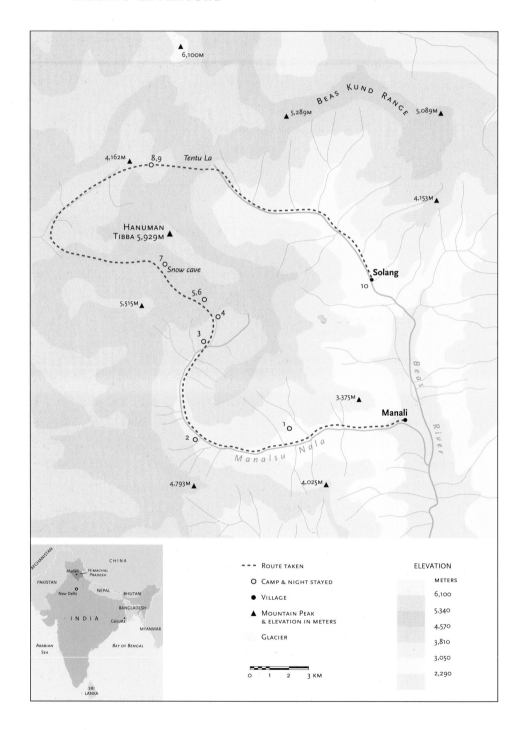

We passed the last buildings on the perimeter of old Manali and began the steep climb up the side of the valley. Our porters, still wearing wool hats and warm jackets, perspired heavily. Soon, however, at a small mountain stream, Amar called for our first break and everyone enjoyed the clear, cool water.

"The porters are wondering why you're on this trip, Sue." Rob had been talking with Amar and had picked up some gossip. "They aren't that used to women doing this kind of thing."

"I know," Sue said. "They think I'm weird. As far as they're concerned, I should be married and have five kids by now. I'm only 29!"

"Our worlds are so different," I said, joining the conversation after taking some photos of our porters.

"We could sure learn a few things from them," Sue said. "Like how to live a less complicated life."

Just then Amar joined us near the stream and addressed Rob. "Our rest is over, sir. We will now continue."

"Thanks, Amar. We'll be right behind you."

We were following the north side of the Manalsu Nala, or river, along a track used by the local people as access to the forests where they gather firewood and drive their herds of goats and cows into the mountains for summer pasturing. The Manalsu Nala isn't a regular trekking route. No one in our group had ever been up the valley and, although Amar had tried the night before in Manali to obtain information about the nature or routing of the track, he had been unsuccessful.

The best map we had been able to find of the area was little more than an artist's impression. At a huge scale of 1:250,000, and an interval of 500 feet between each contour, the map showed few details. Important considerations such as trail locations or terrain features were left to speculation.

We understood the exploratory nature of our trip. As we progressed farther up the valley – and days later into the high mountains – each step of the way, each corner in the distance, every time we crested a rise or gained a pass, each of these moments would hold surprises. Every day of the journey we would commit further to the route, exploring as we went. In an era of E-mail, faxes, instant information, guidebooks, and a feeling that every corner of our planet has seen footprints, it was exhilarating to know that there are still some places where our sense of adventure could lead us to the unknown.

"There is much snow, sir," Amar said as he sipped ice-cold stream water. "It is very far down the mountains."

"There was a lot of snow this year," Rob added, having observed the snowpack all winter with a guide's eye. "It could limit how far the porters will be able to carry our loads."

"Wouldn't it be nice to get two days up the Manalsu Nala?" Sue asked rhetorically. "The closer to the alpine we get before using our skis the better."

Later, where we stopped for lunch, there were extensive patches of snow on the ground; its appearance threatened to put us to work early.

By mid-afternoon our lunchtime concerns were confirmed: snow covered the trail, and our porters weren't pleased with the prospect of plowing ahead with cold feet.

"I'll go first and find the way," Rob said. "You guys come behind and make the steps as easy to follow as you can."

Porters carry their loads up the Manalsu Nala on the first afternoon out of Manali.

Sue looked back at Amar and the porters, who had dropped our packs and were rearranging their loads, then said, "Okay, Rob. But don't get too far in front. These guys don't look too happy about the snow. We may need your help." The grumbling from behind was now quite audible.

Amar's role as *sirdar* was difficult: he knew that it was important to keep us content, but at the same time he had to maintain the respect of the porters. So we kept well ahead of them and left Amar to do his job.

Our next obstacle came when our route up the main river was cut off by the intrusion of a side canyon, halting our forward progress. After an hour of exploring our options, startling a group of 50 or more langur monkeys in the process, we concluded that the only way around the barrier was to follow the gorge uphill until we could skirt across. Unfortunately this would mean more snow and more cold feet for the porters.

Rob set off ahead, forging an uphill track for several hundred meters before finding a way across the canyon. The porters followed grudgingly but maintained a steady pace. Given the conditions and the fact that the porters wore no socks inside rubber boots that scooped more snow than they kept out, we felt fortunate to be moving ahead.

Perseverance paid us dividends, and after two hours of hard climbing through the snow to bypass the canyon obstacle, we happened upon an abandoned shepherd's hut. Next to the hut was a massive, dry rock bathed in the warmth of the evening sun. Soon everyone was enjoying hot soup in the sunset. Looking ahead, we could see that our route dropped to river level and was clear of snow. Amar and the porters came to an agreement that the following day they would carry as far as possible up the valley. Memories of cold feet from earlier in the day were already fading.

March 22 dawned clear and cold. After an early breakfast, we left the hut and made good time up the Manalsu Nala on a clear trail, but by mid-morning we reached a point where the porters could go no farther.

"Thank you for your help." Rob was the main *sahib*, or boss, and he spoke for all of us. "Now it's time for us to ski. We'll see you in one week, Amar."

Each porter received a bonus in recognition of an appreciated special effort in difficult conditions, and Sue added to the tip with handfuls of candy for their long return trek to Manali. One of the porters replied with an exceedingly formal, "Very good, madame." Amar looked ahead to our route into the mountains and asked us to be careful and to "go with God." We watched as our helpers turned their backs and ran unencumbered down the valley.

From here on we would ski – and carry our own packs. So we lifted the heavy loads to our backs and slowly worked our way up the snow-choked valley. The going was tough. Looking ahead, we could see at least a full day of grinding effort before we would climb out of the forest and into the high, open bowls of the alpine. Retreating into the shelter of our individual thoughts, we struggled in frustration, awkwardly thrashing through thickets of alders growing horizontally under the weight of the winter's snow. The eight-day cargo on our backs was a further hindrance, one that always required time to get used to.

Two difficult hours later we took a much-needed break for a drink and a bite to eat. We each offered to produce the food for lunch, looking for any chance to

Amar eats dinner on the first night.

lighten our load. But despite the hard work, we were enjoying the sense of moving forward. The character of the area was gradually shifting from subalpine to alpine, and we were climbing into the high mountains and glaciated terrain that was the object of our journey. Peaks still rose thousands of meters above us, but our progress was noticeable. With some fuel in our bodies we set off rested and energized, allowing our curiosity about what we might find just around the corner to draw us into the unknown.

Our route continued along the course of the Manalsu Nala. Travel improved as we moved upriver, and with so much of the deep valley filled in with snow, we skied right up the middle. Then, less than an hour after lunch, the way began to constrict, and it was apparent that our only route was through a steeply walled, narrow gorge where the river flowed in summer. Rising above the gorge were huge snow slopes that funneled right into the canyon.

We stopped and talked about the hazard before entering the gorge, trying our best to assess the risk. "That's quite a feature," Rob volunteered. "I'd say that's pretty much the definition of a terrain trap."

"No kidding, Rob. What a grim spot." My comment expressed what we all felt. None of us wanted to go through the slot. Between us we had more than 40 years of mountain travel experience; that experience disciplines the mountaineer to avoid such obvious dangers. However, we could see no realistic route option, and our observations suggested that the snow conditions were relatively stable. There were no signs of new avalanche activity, and we suspected that the warm temperatures of spring had consolidated the lower snowpack, eliminating deep instabilities that might have been lingering from the winter storms. Our judgment was that the hazard was slight, and we elected to go through the gorge.

Still apprehensive, we moved cautiously, spreading out for safety, hoping that if an avalanche occurred perhaps only one of us would be hit and the others could still carry out a rescue. The threat from above created a nervous feeling in the pits of our stomachs. There was no denying the potential danger as we skied over old avalanche debris that was probably several meters thick. Although we had logically deduced that the risk was acceptable, no decision is ever without its doubts. Fear kept us alert and moving steadily through the gorge.

61

FOLLOWING PAGES: *Sunset on Deo Tibba, a 6,000-meter peak across the Beas Valley, on the first night of the trip up the Manalsu Nala.*

Rob had already passed the hazard, and I stopped for a moment to take a picture of Sue. "Hey, Sue!" I yelled ahead to catch her attention. "I'll get a shot of you skiing near the rock."

Just after I pressed the shutter release, I heard Sue shout, "Jim!"

I was frightened into panic. "Avalanche!" I screamed. Snow thundered over the cliffs and hammered into the gorge behind me. With my camera still in both hands and my poles dangling from my wrists, I shuffled awkwardly ahead like a hobbled donkey. I had always imagined that if I ever had to escape an avalanche on skis it would be in an adrenaline-driven tuck through deep powder, but here I was tripping over old frozen lumps of snow, heading uphill in a confined canyon. The only parallel between my dreams and the reality of this crisis was the adrenaline; my heart raced and blood pounded in my ears.

As the sound of the avalanche eased, and my chemically inspired heart rate dropped toward normal, I glanced around to see a small slide of snow finishing its run over the cliffs and smothering the old debris in the bottom of the gorge. I put my camera away and focused on getting out of there. It was a small but dramatic reminder of where we were and the dire consequences of a mistake.

By late afternoon we were safely past the avalanche threat, and the temperature had dropped noticeably. Worn out after our day carrying heavy loads, we pitched our tents in the lee of a snowbank, effectively sheltering our camp from the steady wind whipping down the valley. A quick change into warm clothing helped ward off the chill of the evening air. Our stove began to hum after extensive priming, a necessary step when the only camping fuel that you can buy in India is low-grade kerosene. The intention was to melt snow for our first of many hot drinks.

Our camp that night was at 3,200 meters, more than 1,000 meters above Manali, and we noted the beginning of a process that takes several days – the adaptation of our bodies to higher altitudes. The summit of Hanuman Tibba rises to 5,940 meters, so it was important that we gradually acclimatize; to complete the tour through the Beas Kund, we would have to camp several nights at 5,000 meters or higher.

The following morning brought clear skies and cold air – the temperature had dropped overnight to -10 degrees Celsius – and we set off up the breathtaking

*Sue skis among the avalanche debris in the narrow gorge
on the second day of our tour.*

valley ahead with very little idea of what to expect. We were above the tree line, and the open alpine country seemed to give us a lift.

"What a view!" Sue said as we crested a small rise. "When the weather's like this, it's as though you can reach out and touch the mountains. It's gorgeous."

"It's great to see the route ahead," Rob said as he pulled the map out of his pack. "Straight up the valley until we can see what's around the corner looks good to me."

We traveled up this broad valley, marveling at the beauty of the high peaks and taking photographs of the steep granite walls as we skied beside them.

By late morning the weather began to change. Clouds rolled in from the south and visibility deteriorated. We could make out a route up a side valley that would give access to the upper icefields near Hanuman Tibba, and although we were quite sure it would be safe for most of the way, the clouds obscured the upper portion. Once again we were reminded of the uncertain element of our adventure. The map was little help, so we decided not to gamble and continued up the main valley. Even though it was longer, the primary drainage of the Manalsu Nala appeared to offer the most consistent terrain and, in our judgment, seemed to have the fewest potential obstacles.

Snow began to fall lightly in the middle of the afternoon. As the day darkened and visibility was reduced to near zero, we elected to set up camp on the glacier at 4,350 meters, 12 kilometers from our previous camp. Now altitude was having a noticeable effect on our bodies: our movements became sluggish and energy levels decreased. It no longer felt like spring: falling snow and frigid winds brought back cold memories of winter. It took two hours to set up camp – shoveling snow and building a wall – and once that job was done we crawled gratefully into our tents to escape the weather.

We carried two tents with us: Sue and I in our small two-person shelter and Rob alone in his tiny Gore-Tex sanctuary. In bad weather we pitched the tents with the doors facing each other so we could communicate and pass food from one tent to the other.

The unpredictable weather, common in the spring in the Himalayas, produced a glorious morning on March 24. Soft light highlighted the new snow shrouding the peaks, but the clear skies brought colder temperatures. It was difficult to get motivated when the thermometer read -12 degrees Celsius and our down sleeping bags were still warm and cozy. It took until 9:00 a.m. to get ready to leave the campsite. Our solitary track up the center of the glacier, barely visible, was all that disturbed the previous night's fresh snow.

Clouds began to build slowly as the day heated up. Soon snow was falling in earnest and visibility was again reduced to just a few meters. A fiercely cold wind whipped snow in our faces. Travel was at first uncomfortable, then it became dangerous. Skiing on a glacier in the springtime is a normal event, but it requires good visibility because of the hazard of crevasses. By noon it was obvious that we couldn't go any farther in the face of the building storm. Carefully probing for crevasses, we pitched the tents at an exposed spot in the middle of the glacier, as far as possible from any avalanche slopes.

We had climbed quickly, and I wasn't surprised to read on my altimeter that we had reached 5,000 meters. Now, more than ever, we were aware of the effects of altitude on our bodies: shortness of breath and slow movement. Sue had a bad headache and was feeling nauseous. She knelt in the tent, clasped her head in her hands, and groaned from the discomfort. Grimacing at the thought of eating or drinking anything, she managed to swallow two tablets of Ibuprofin. Within 15 minutes she had curled up on her side, with a relaxed smile on her face.

Rob and I immediately went to work to raise a snow wall to protect our camp, and as soon as the job was finished, we piled into our respective tents. A sandwich and a bowl of soup for lunch made the blizzard seem a bit less intimidating. A soothing mug of tea followed, and we turned to reading for the remainder of the afternoon. Sue and I were each enjoying tales of travel in Tibet: she was reading Vikram Seth's *From Heaven Lake,* while Heinrich Harrer's classic, *Seven Years in Tibet,* helped me pass my afternoon. Sue now felt much better as her body continued to adapt to the altitude. Outside, the weather worsened. The barometer continued to drop, the winds roared with greater ferocity from the south, and the snowfall became heavier. Several signs of a severe mountain storm were on display.

On March 25 we awoke with mouthfuls of tent. The snow that had fallen throughout the night had accumulated in such quantity that it had compressed the sides of our tents into our faces. In fact, the level of the snow deposited out-side was at the height of the wall we had built the previous day. The remains of the wall still deflected the brunt of the wind, but the snow carried by the gale was piling up on the lee side. It had all but filled our walled compound. An hour's worth of shoveling was needed to clear the tents, then it took another hour to raise the wall against the increasing rage of the storm.

The rest of that day passed slowly. The nylon walls of a tent, although pro-viding crucial protection from the uncharitable elements, always seem restrict-ing during the long hours of a storm day. There is little to do except read, drink plenty of fluids, and be ready to go, both mentally and physically, should the weather improve. The big events on tent-bound storm days are meals and the ordeal of going to the toilet. Meals are a highlight, anticipated hours in advance. Trips outside to an open-air bathroom involve leaving a warm sleeping bag and getting completely dressed in damp clothing to face the fury of the wind.

By late afternoon it had become apparent that there would be no skiing that day, and we waited impatiently for the day's remaining events: first dinner, then darkness and the excuse to sleep.

I woke up at about midnight, vaguely aware that something was wrong but too groggy with sleep to know exactly what was happening. I groped for my flashlight in the darkness. As my head cleared, I realized that our shelter was again smoth-ered under the weight of the fresh snow. I hit the side of the tent in an attempt to push back the snow, but it was like smashing my fist into a heavy punching bag. Nothing moved.

"Sue," I whispered, trying to be gentle, "wake up."

"What's up? What time is it?" She was still in dreamland.

"It's just past midnight. Our tent is totally smothered by the snow. I've got to go out and take a look. Can you give me a hand?"

"Okay. Just give me a minute."

The snow was so deep that I had to dig my way out of the tent. As I stood, the wind lashed my face; the cold temperature and the ice crystals driven by the storm shocked me instantly alert and drove any night weariness from my head. I could see only as far as the beam from my headlamp into the darkness. Big flakes of snow reflected brightly in the shaft of light and drove horizontally past me. The mass of accumulated snow had buried both tents. I fastened all of my clothing tightly and began digging us out. Alone in the dark, I found myself curiously mesmerized by the beam of my headlamp and settled into a trancelike state as my body became absorbed by the repetitive drudgery of moving snow.

As I shoveled, I pondered our predicament. We were in a wild mountain location in northern India in a severe winter storm, days from any help. I felt strangely comfortable with this thought, probably because the situation still seemed manageable. I thought about the natural world – how it lets us travel among its different environments, allows us passage over its glaciers and onto its high summits, sharing the wind, the magnificent vistas, and the warmth of the sun. We enjoy a type of intimacy with nature in these places. But maybe intimacy is too strong a word. The association is really a matter of nature's acceptance of our modest efforts and our vanities, and every once in a while it startles us with a forceful reminder of the true character of the relationship. I had to shovel now or risk losing the tent, which was a horrible thought.

Once the camp was clear of snow I ducked back inside. I was covered in ice – plastered on my face and clothing by the wind – and needed to crawl into my sleeping bag and warm up. Outside, the wind continued and the falling snow persevered in its relentless objective to bury our campsite. It was just after 1:30 a.m. We set the alarm for 4:00 a.m. so we could get up to check the amount of snow on the tent. After that, sleep came easily.

When the alarm rang it was dark, and the storm outside was still howling. The quantity of snow accumulating on our camp hardly seemed enough to justify getting out of a warm sleeping bag, so I dropped back into a heavy sleep. But by 7:00 a.m. the tents were in trouble again. This time it was Rob and Sue's turn, and they dug their way out of the trapped tents and engineered the rescue of our camp. Between spells of digging they fired up the stove and started the morning brew.

Snow fell steadily all morning, and it was clear that March 26, our sixth day since leaving Manali, was going to bring more enforced rest. We reevaluated our original plan of a seven-day ski tour. There was no longer a chance of completing the route in that time frame; in a best-case scenario we needed two days of skiing

The view of our tent from Rob's tent during the storm on
March 26, 1995. Photo: Rob Orvig.

to reach the village of Solang, but with the quantity of new snow it would more than likely take three days. Our hope of climbing Hanuman Tibba along the way was fading – we still hadn't even *seen* the mountain. We had started out with eight days' worth of food, and although we had been carefully rationing our supplies, they were dwindling. The day was spent listening to fresh snow avalanches cascade off the surrounding peaks, and we continued shoveling out our campsite, which now resembled an enormous bathtub with walls almost two meters deep.

By evening the storm showed signs of abating; snow stopped falling and in the distance peaks poked through the clouds. By midnight the sky had cleared and the thermometer plunged. It was -21 degrees Celsius at daybreak. When sunlight hit our campsite two hours later, it was a welcome relief: the warmth helped to thaw our cold fingers and toes. The peaks were swathed in fresh snow from the storm's effort, and the fantastic sculptures created by the wind glistened in the subtle morning light. Sue, who was the first to surface, managed the final act of snow removal from the tents and started the stove for breakfast.

I ventured out of our shoveled compound and quickly found myself wallowing up to my chest in loose snow. "Look at how deep this is!" I howled to no one in particular.

Five minutes later Rob followed my trench to answer nature's call. "This isn't so bad," he said with a smile. "I'm only up to my waist."

Sue found Rob's remark more amusing than I, but after 30 years of jokes about my height, I was used to such friendly barbs.

We decided to go ahead with our original plan, counting on good weather in the next few days. It seemed too soon to turn back; the lure of what was just around the corner drew us on. I began breaking trail in the mid-morning sunshine, but my skis sank up past my knees into the fresh snow, making travel with a heavy pack simply too difficult. I dropped my load and set off. Liberated, I plowed a track for Rob and Sue to follow and found it workable. My plan was to ski for an hour or so, then return on the established track to get my gear.

The beautiful morning and the activity after being pinned inside a tent revitalized us. Breaking trail was arduous, but the exhilarating views of the peaks provided a powerful distraction. Sharp, dramatic ridges swept off the glacier to barblike summits. Between the ridges, frozen rock faces sheathed in storm-driven snow provided thoughts of future climbing objectives. There were signs of new snow avalanches everywhere – dozens of tracks where the snow had run during the storm. And the wind had fashioned frozen waves of snow on the glacier for miles around us.

After a couple of hours of hard work, we turned a corner in the glacier to see the bulk of Hanuman Tibba rising in front of us. We had reached 5,300 meters, the high point of our skiing route. The weather was perfect. We ate lunch at the base of the mountain and decided to camp there, hoping to climb to the summit early the following morning. After that we would follow our original plan and head out to Solang through the Beas Kund. With the knowledge that everything was back on track, we basked in the afternoon sun. From a logistical perspective we could stretch our food to last two days, our fuel – crucial for melting snow for water – would last four days, and if the warm daytime weather continued, the fresh snow avalanche hazard would settle quickly.

"Let's dig a cave here," Rob suggested. "I was freezing last night in my tent."

"Sure, Rob. Great idea," I said. "We could put the entrance right here by this wind roll."

Snow is an excellent insulator, and the inside of a cave can be 0 degrees Celsius even when the outside temperature is well below freezing. Building a snow cave is a long, involved process, but once finished it provides genuine security from any onslaught of weather. After we finished the snow cave, we ate dinner by sunset, then went to bed early, anticipating a predawn start to climb Hanuman Tibba.

At 4:00 a.m. I slid out of the entrance to our cave and immediately realized there would be no summit attempt. It was snowing lightly, but a more ominous sign was the temperature – only -4 degrees Celsius. A warm front was approaching. We packed up, and by 6:30 a.m. we were standing on our skis trying to decide whether to go on to Solang or to retrace our route to Manali.

We wanted to complete the journey. The route had never been skied, and our desire to explore the way before us was a big attraction. But removing personal feelings such as ego, pride, and ambition from the process was a major part of the challenge of going to such a place. It was time to be as objective as possible. Our food and fuel were limited, and the weather was again deteriorating. Which way to go?

"We don't know anything about the way ahead," Sue reminded us.

"It's much shorter than going back to Manali," I offered. "And with all this fresh snow, going back through that canyon doesn't appeal to me at all."

Rob summarized the two options. "Both ways have potentially dangerous sections. The descent through the Beas Kund is steep and could be hazardous. If we turn back now, we know the route. But it'll take two or three days and will also mean walking down the trail all the way to Manali. Solang is still in the snow and we'll be able to ski right into the village."

"It's only one or two days to Solang," I said.

"*If* the route into the Beas Kund works," Sue countered.

"I think we should go for it," I said, still wanting to finish the tour.

"Okay," Rob said.

"All right then. Let's go," Sue added, making the decision unanimous. Her words committed us to the route ahead, and as the snow fell more steadily, we skied forward toward the Beas Kund.

On March 27, 1995, after the storm, Rob works with his shovel to excavate our camp at 5,000 meters. Unnamed peaks of the Indian Himalayas extend to the south.

It was 7:00 a.m. From this point on our tour would be downhill, except for one more climb of 500 meters to the Tentu La, the pass to the north of Hanuman Tibba that separated us from the Beas Kund. Gravity would be on our side everywhere else. If the terrain was moderate, if the avalanche hazard in the Beas Kund wasn't too high, and if the weather stayed reasonably clear, then we might make it safely to the forest by nightfall. From there it was only 15 kilometers down the valley of the Beas River to Solang.

The surface of the snow was crusty from the previous day's sunshine, and the skiing was difficult. At the bottom of a big hill I lost control of my skis in the poor snow and fell. I shouted up to Sue that conditions weren't great and watched helplessly as she gained speed in the track Rob and I had made and then crashed hard at the bottom, twisting her back. Our initial fears of a serious injury were quickly banished, but the idea of a broken bone or torn ligament in such a place made us all ski with added caution.

The weather wasn't on our side. By the time we reached the flat section on the glacier where we would have to turn east and climb to the Tentu La, it was snowing heavily and visibility was reduced to just a few meters. We put our climbing skins back on our skis and began feeling our way up the side glacier toward the pass. The wind whipped the clouds across the sky, only occasionally allowing us glimpses of our surroundings. We realized that this valley was much more constricted than we had expected, with huge mountain walls rising above us on either side. Our route would have to follow the middle of the glacier as much as possible to avoid any avalanches crashing down from above.

The higher we climbed toward the Tentu La, the worse the weather became. My altimeter read 4,800 meters at just after noon. The pass was only another 200 meters above us, but travel was getting more difficult. Our skis penetrated more than 20 centimeters into the fresh snow, extracting ever-increasing amounts of energy from our weary bodies.

While I was breaking trail, Rob confided to Sue, "I think we made the wrong decision to go forward. We should have returned to Manali. At least we knew that terrain."

"Especially given the grim weather," Sue said.

"And our lack of food," Rob added.

Our confidence was eroding and all three of us were tiring quickly. Rob had been fighting a flulike bug, which was now dragging him deeper into fatigue. With the wind driving snow hard into our faces, visibility was zero. The route through the Tentu La would be tricky. It was the most technical aspect of the entire trip and we needed to see where we were going; both for route selection and hazard analysis. Fresh snow avalanches were beginning to pound down Hanuman Tibba, echoing very near and producing an eerie sound through the clouds.

"Those are too close," Rob said, alarmed by the rumble of the last avalanche.

"I'm not sure how far we are from Hanuman Tibba," I said, "but I don't want to get too close to the other side, either." I was leading the way and felt as if I were inside a Ping-Pong ball: it was a total whiteout, and there was no reference to up or down except the few meters of our track that we could see behind us.

After a brief conference, we decided to work our way into the middle of the glacier and find a high point on which to set up camp. It was an all too familiar routine as we dug in to wait out another storm.

Avalanches, sounding like trains rumbling past in the night, continued at regular intervals. "Do you think those slides will reach us?" Sue asked, searching for some comforting assurance.

"We're safe on this high point," I replied with unfounded confidence.

Rob said nothing, but I knew he wished we could see exactly where we had chosen to pitch our tents.

Our eighth day on the trip meant we had reached our last day of food. We were camped at 4,950 meters, and again the wind howled and the snow fell relentlessly. We had two days of fuel left for melting snow. If we had retreated from the snow cave down the Manalsu Nala, we would still be descending, possibly making our way into the forest by nightfall.

"There's not much left for dinner, guys," I said as I surveyed the remnants in the food bag. "We have some pasta, a soup package, and a bunch of those dried soy balls."

"Only soup and pasta for me," Rob said in a muffled voice from the other tent. "I'm sick of those barf balls!"

"We're out of cookies," Sue informed us as she rummaged through the dessert bag. "It's time to go home." At least we were maintaining our sense of humor.

At 5:00 a.m. on March 29 I was again forced outside into a storm to shovel new snow off the tents. It took more than an hour to rescue our camp. Avalanches thundered down the steep north face of Hanuman Tibba, yet all I could see were the clouds and blowing snow in front of my face. I crawled back into our tent, wondering how long we would remain prisoners of the weather.

We had essentially run out of food. What was left we rationed in the hope that it would see us out of the mountains. Our spirits were sagging. Frustration with the weather and apprehension of what lay ahead – not knowing what the descent from the Tentu La would be like – left each of us slightly irritable. Sue's back was sore from her fall the previous day, and we were hungry. However, there was nothing to do except be patient and wait for the opportunity to escape. The insides of our tents were becoming much too familiar as the day passed uneventfully.

The unpredictable weather pattern continued on March 30, our 10th day since leaving Manali. We woke up early in the morning to a cloudless sky and an extremely low temperature. It was -22 degrees Celsius, and for the first time we could clearly see where we were camped. We had chosen well: a high knoll in the center of the valley, safe from avalanches. Another meter of fresh snow had fallen, covering the entire area with a clean white coat that contrasted brilliantly with the blue sky. Unfortunately our hunger and cold toes dominated our thoughts so that the full effect of our dramatic surroundings ran a distant second in our minds. The priority was to get out of the mountains and do it safely. Rob and I set off toward the Tentu La without packs to explore route options while Sue got our damp gear into the sunlight to dry out.

We skied toward the pass in knee-deep snow. For both of us a combination of hunger and altitude – and flulike symptoms for Rob – produced a queasy lethargy. Although there was plenty of fresh snow on the glacier, the mountain faces appeared to have shed their new snow in the form of avalanches during the storm. As Rob and I reached the Tentu La and looked down for the first time into the Beas Kund, both of us were startled by the abruptness of the terrain. It dropped precipitously for more than 1,500 meters.

76

Poised at the top of the Beas Kund in the Tentu La,
Rob contemplates the 2,000-meter descent
into the valley below.

"Look at how far down it goes," I said. Without a quality map I was taken by surprise at the scale of the descent. "It's steep."

"What about the hazard?" Rob asked.

"I think everything's run already. The slopes are too steep to hold such a big storm. As long as it stays cool, we should be okay."

"Let's be quick about it," Rob said, peering down the slopes of the Beas Kund. "Who knows when the next storm will come." As we left the top to return to camp and help Sue with the job of packing, he added, "We won't want to spend too long under those faces. We'll have to move quickly."

Three hours later, when we returned to the 5,100-meter-high pass with Sue, the clouds had again moved in and visibility had deteriorated to near zero. Fortunately these clouds were only associated with the heat of the day and weren't a storm system, so it only served to make the travel more difficult, not unsafe.

"The anchor's ready, Rob! You're on belay!" I shouted so I could be heard above the rising wind. "Sue! You'll have to watch him for me. I can't see the edge from here."

"I'm on my way!" Rob yelled back. "I'll check out the snow, then we'll see you at the bottom."

"Good luck, Rob!" Sue hollered from her perch overlooking the first 100 meters of the slope, which was at a 40-degree angle and still seemed to hold some storm snow. Rob would stay on belay while he dug a pit in the snow so he could determine the avalanche hazard.

"He's disappearing into the clouds!" Sue yelled. "But he waved up and indicated it looked okay. He's gone down."

"Let's get going," I said as I took the belay apart. By the time Sue and I had worked our way out of the windswept Tentu La and down the initial sheer slopes from the col, all that we could see of Rob's passage was a deep track leading away into the mist. We followed.

From there we skied steep gullies and faces, slowly fighting our way toward the valley floor. The final gully was a dark cleft more than 800 meters long, only 25 meters wide and tilted at an angle of 35 degrees – very steep. All of the signs we had observed, and data we had gathered, suggested that conditions were safe

78

Rob gazes at Hanuman Tibba and dreams of the peak we never got a chance to climb. This was the 10th and final day of our ski tour.

to enter such a place. Our decision was to go for it. Instinctively we knew how important committing to such a route was: there was no escape.

"This snow is brutal," I panted. The observation was obvious. "It looks like kick turns from here."

Sue was particularly frustrated with the unskiable snow, since we still hadn't really skied on the entire trip. Essentially we had toiled uphill from Manali to the Tentu La, and our big descent had become a tiring series of traverses and kick turns. Our track made it seem as if Zorro had spent the day practicing his famous mark.

"This is crazy and I'm tired," Sue said matter-of-factly.

"Keep your eyes peeled for an avalanche from above, Sue, and ski hard to the wall of the gully if you see one." I was all business. "And ski conservatively. We don't want an injury here."

"Just get going. I'll be behind you."

I frequently glanced over my shoulder to reassure myself about our judgment. The whole gully was covered in avalanche debris, and I shuddered when I thought about how much snow had poured down from above only 24 hours earlier.

An hour later we were out of the gully and into the sunshine in the basin of the Beas Kund. It felt great to be gliding along the surface of the snow, gaining distance from the huge face behind us with every passing minute. It also felt wonderful to be closing the gap between us and civilization at the same rate. Rob sat on his pack, waiting patiently. Together again, we zipped down to the forest and reached the road beside the Beas River just as the sun dipped behind the ridge to the west. All that remained in our journey was the final 15 kilometers of snow-covered road to Solang.

Sitting on our packs, we ate our last morsels of food and stared back at the Tentu La more than 2,000 meters above, aware of just how tired we were. Although the last stage of our tour was relatively simple, it would take all our energy. Wearily we lifted our packs and pushed off slowly down the road.

Eventually the day faded toward night, and the dull light of dusk changed to darkness. We were still skiing, too exhausted to stop and camp, too hungry to consider that as an option. It was warm here in the valley, the snow was frustratingly sloppy, and under the weight of our packs we were actually hot and sweaty for the first time in more than a week.

"Sue!" I called out, drawing her attention from the beam of her headlamp, which was focused on the snow. "There's the Friendship Hotel. I can see the lights."

"Thank God!" was all she could muster.

At 9:00 p.m. on March 30 we arrived in Solang, familiar ground for Sue and me since we had spent two nights there earlier in our travels.

"Welcome, my friends," Mr. Metha, the owner of the hotel, said. He had heard us arrive and hurried out to receive us with a big smile and open arms. The locals were incredulous when we told them we had skied from Manali to Solang via the Beas Kund. However, we were too tired to explain our adventure in any detail; our main focus was dinner.

Waiting for food to come from the dimly lit kitchen in the back of the hotel, we sought out the warmth of the big wood-burning stove in the center of the sitting room.

"Rob. Sue. You want a Coke?" I had been thinking about a cold drink all the way down the road.

Their positive response was simultaneous, and we drained two Cokes each before switching to the locally bottled apple juice. It all tasted so good that it seemed impossible to slow down. Dinner arrived and we feasted on the standard fare of rice, lentils, and curry sauce. After eating, we went directly to our rooms and fell fast asleep in beds with fresh sheets and soft quilts.

I dragged myself out of bed the following day, joints creaking, and gazed out the window at the high peaks surrounding Solang, already bathed in mid-morning sunshine. They looked friendly and inviting, their character changed once again. But I knew otherwise. I had felt their strength and struggled with their temperament. It had been a challenging journey, much more difficult than I had expected, but the treasure of the experience was fair compensation.

All that remained was to return by road to Manali. After a pancake-and-honey breakfast, we left the Friendship Hotel, hopped on the back of a tractor bound for town, and bounced the final 20 kilometers of our trip into the crowded streets of

Manali. In the low valley the sun was hot, and the colorful stalls lining the street were laden with fruit and vegetables. It looked and felt like spring. We walked the final hill to the office of Himalayan Journeys and found Amar and his cohorts sitting outside the door, patiently waiting for the summer trekking season to arrive. It was still two months away.

As we entered the office, our packs were eased off our backs and glasses of steaming hot chai appeared from nowhere. There were many questions and laughter, and general excitement. Then we learned that Amar had been to Solang two days earlier and had been asking if anyone had seen or heard anything of our whereabouts. Rob asked him if he had been worried, and he simply replied, "No, sir. I knew for you and a man who has climbed K2 it would be no problem."

Sunrise on the peaks above Solang.

ROOF OF AFRICA
Clandestine Adventures on Mounts Kenya and Kilimanjaro

THE RULES ARE CLEAR. Common sense really. In the Third World countries of Africa there are some things you simply don't do. For instance, you keep your mouth shut in the shower because the parasites and amoebas that commonly swim in tap water thrive and multiply in your stomach. And eating with your left hand will earn you scowls and frowns, since many Africans consider such conduct uncivilized in a land where toilet paper is usually a luxury and the left hand has certain duties. But challenging authority, particularly if that authority is toting a gun, is downright dangerous.

Eric Boyum, my longtime climbing friend from Canada, and I were in East Africa in January in the last days of the Cold War, tolerating a long list of questions from a grouchy park warden, when a bright flash of light exploded in the room. I spun around to see a tall, scruffy, bearded man holding a camera to which a big flash unit was attached. Unbelievably he was refocusing for a second shot. Every travel book on the shelf advises not to take pictures of "official" things like bridges, airports, and army personnel. This person was clearly taking a chance.

The warden's eyes blazed with anger, and instinctively I stepped aside to let the two adversaries meet. The photographer lowered his camera and returned the official's gaze with a big smile and an apologetic expression. In broken English and a heavy Slavic accent, he asked forgiveness. Using these techniques, the photographer managed to convince the warden that he hadn't threatened the man's absolute grip on local power. A potential crisis calmed and the photographer had his picture. If he had first asked permission, it would surely have been denied.

Sunset on Kilimanjaro, Africa's highest peak at 5,895 meters.

That's how I met Miroslav Šmid, a wild and talented Czech mountain climber, as he tempted the patience of an armed park warden at the entrance to Mount Kenya National Park.

East Africa is a fabled region that has attracted explorers, romantics, and adventurers for centuries. Many have come seeking treasure or fame. Some have left ruin in their wake. To most anthropologists, this is where humanity's earliest ancestors first evolved, and where today the lions, elephants, rhinoceroses, wildebeests, gazelles, zebras, leopards, cheetahs, and countless other animals found here are the most visible and dramatic examples of the delicate relationship between predator and prey. And then there are the people. From proud Masai herdsmen to the powerful Samburu, the present-day inhabitants of East Africa are unique and memorable, invoking visions of timeless vistas peopled with ancient tribes.

This is a primeval land. The great Rift Valley, a vast geological gash, runs the entire length of the African continent. The huge inland lakes of Victoria, Tanganyika, and Turkana give life and spawn hope for the future. The greatest mountains on the continent – the Ruwenzori and Mounts Kenya and Kilimanjaro – are dramatic snowcapped giants rising above hot equatorial plains. Clearly there is too much to explore and investigate within any person's lifetime.

After signing in and paying our park entrance fees, Eric and I clambered into the back of the daily truck from Nanyuki, a small town on the west side of Mount Kenya. Our destination was the meteorological station and the trailhead. Several African workers occupied benches along the walls of the truck box waiting for the *muzungu,* Kiswahili slang for "white people," to finish their business at the gate. The Czech threw his heavy load into the back of the truck and climbed up, reaching back to help his partner with his pack. The two men settled in across the box from Eric and me and introductions followed.

Fritz Roth was from Switzerland, and his English was excellent. He and his friend, Miri, had come to climb Mount Kenya before heading south to Tanzania for an attempt on Kilimanjaro. They had only three weeks in East Africa and hoped to visit one or more of the great game parks as well. Just then the big diesel truck abruptly coughed, and the continuous rumbling of the unmuffled engine cut off our conversation.

A lone impala in the evening mist on the Serengeti Plain.

The rutted road combined with the truck's stiff suspension to produce a bumpy 90-minute ride through the dense bamboo forest that completely surrounds Mount Kenya. But the practical result of this uncomfortable drive, besides saving energy, was that we were spared any unexpected encounters with unpredictable animals such as elephants, lions, Cape buffalos, or leopards, which make their home in the thickets.

From the trailhead it was two days' hiking to reach the base of the mountain. The track was gradual, perfect for progressively increasing fitness and acclimatization. Mount Kenya is almost 5,200 meters high, and we knew it would take several days for our bodies to adjust to the altitude. The mountain is a large, central type volcano, built up by intermittent eruptions more than 2.5 million years ago. The base of the volcano is more than 100 kilometers in diameter, and originally its summit must have reached well over 6,500 meters. Mount Kenya's present appearance can be attributed to timeless erosion from rain, wind, snow, and the many glaciers imperceptibly carving its face.

On January 17 we pitched our tent at 4,400 meters in the meadows of the American Camp below the impressive South Face of Mount Kenya. Sharing the grassy campsite with us were Miri and Fritz.

Eric and I had climbed together for years; we had shared ascents on remote peaks in British Columbia's Coast Mountains and classic climbs in the Canadian Rockies. Now, to acclimatize ourselves for the summit climb, we walked to the top of Point Lenana, a subpeak of Mount Kenya, then ascended the standard route up the main summit – a technical, enjoyable rock climb. Only two meters below the pinnacle of the summit, we were astonished to find a tiny bivouac shelter. Constructed of wood and aluminum and firmly anchored to the rock with taut guy wires, this refuge is certainly one of the more memorable mountain huts in the world. It was built in 1970 by local climber Ian Howell who, in a prodigious effort in February of that year, made 13 solo ascents of the mountain, carrying all of the materials to the summit on his back. Eric and I poked our heads inside the dark, tiny shack and decided it would be a welcome spot to spend the night if we were late; but there was still plenty of time left in our day, so we began the descent. By the 19th we were feeling fit and ready for a route on the steep face that loomed above camp.

89

The steep South Face of Mount Kenya from the Teleki Valley. The Diamond Couloir splits the face and is probably the finest climbing line on the mountain. Its near-vertical icefall drops directly from the lip of the Diamond Glacier, a rock-hard pocket of ice nestled between the twin summits – Nelion and Batian – of the mountain.

We had planned to climb the famous Diamond Couloir on the South Face, but a heavy accumulation of storm snow on the route warned of the possibility of dangerous avalanche conditions, so we settled for the safer Ice Window Route. Awakening on January 20 at 4:30 a.m., we breakfasted quickly on hot chocolate and fruitcake and left camp quietly by headlamp. Two hours later, having crossed the hard ice of the Darwin Glacier, we reached the base of the route. A narrow gash in the rock, full of blue-green water ice, split the face above. It looked intimidating. Our crampons cut through the veneer of ice, searching for purchase on the rocks, a tenuous game at best. After 50 meters the frozen water thickened comfortably and we began to move efficiently up the ice.

Clouds swirled around the face, moving in and out, limiting visibility. The climbing was superb. Eric and I swung leads up the steep terrain, our productive teamwork speeding the ascent. Fourteen rope lengths brought us to the summit of Mount Kenya. Classic. It was just after noon and snow was threatening, so we began our descent.

Despite the clouds, our previous climb of the standard route now made the descent familiar. Thirteen hours after leaving the American Camp we crossed the meadow to our tent. As we were taking off our boots and changing into clean clothes, Miri arrived at our site with a big pot of tea. Fritz was close behind with biscuits. We told our story of the Ice Window climb, and Fritz, a mountain guide by profession, quizzed us for details of the route, explaining that they were planning to tackle it the next day. We were enthusiastic about our accomplishment, an excitement fueled by their interest. The four of us shared other stories as we cooked dinner, then each of us slipped into our sleeping bags shortly after dark. Eric and I fell asleep easily.

We had a lazy morning, rising late to enjoy the warm sunrise in the meadow. Our entertainment was Fritz and Miri, who were already high on the South Face by 9:00 a.m. To our surprise they weren't climbing the Ice Window, after all, but had switched to the Diamond Couloir. Following their progress through binoculars, we could see that they were climbing without a rope, moving quickly up the steep ice. By noon they reached the Gate of the Mists, the prominent gap between Nelion and Batian, the twin summits of Mount Kenya that had been

*Eric uses crampons and ice tools to grapple with the steep ice of the Ice
Window Route on Mount Kenya's South Face.*

named after Masai chieftains by British geographer H. J. MacKinder when he made the first recorded ascent of the mountain in September 1899. Above the gap, afternoon clouds cloaked the mountain and Fritz and Miri disappeared from view.

When they returned to camp at 6:00 p.m., we had the opportunity to repay the previous day's favor by offering tea and cookies as they sat to remove their boots. They had indeed climbed the Diamond Couloir unroped, and Miri showed us the tools he had used – they were made of titanium and came from the Soviet Union. The bizarre devices, one held in each hand, looked fittingly like a cross between a scythe and a meat hook. They were quite different from the traditional ice axes that Fritz, Eric, and I used.

"Is good. Strong," said Miri when I asked him how well they worked on the steep ice.

It snowed that night and continued the following morning, so we decided that it was time to leave Mount Kenya. Eric and I chose to traverse the mountain and hike out via the Chogoria Valley to the east. Miri and Fritz would retrace their approach steps down the MacKinder Valley to Nanyuki for a quick exit and the possibility of a game safari before going on to Tanzania to attempt Mount Kilimanjaro. We exchanged addresses, and Miri gave Eric and me each a present of a Soviet titanium ice screw. I promised Miri I would do what I could to get him an official invitation to climb in Canada. In those days, before Czechoslovakia's Velvet Revolution, such invitations cut through the bureaucracy that East Europeans faced when applying for exit permits for a climbing vacation in the West.

Eric's vacation was nearly over, and he would leave in a couple of days for Canada. A month still remained of my holiday, but I had no concrete plans about how I would spend that time. I thought of a return visit to the tropical shores of Kenya. The idea of snorkeling and exploring the coast was appealing, particularly when I thought about the warm waters of the Indian Ocean and the Muslim influence of centuries of Arabic seafarers who had used the reliable seasonal winds to travel and trade on the east coast of Africa. The region is rich with history. Another alternative was an overland truck ride to the northern border of Kenya near Ethiopia, a land of mostly volcanic desert, hot and unforgiving. The Turkana,

Rendille, Gabbra, and El Molo people of that region are quite different from any other inhabitants of East Africa. I daydreamed about these possibilities as Eric and I ambled along Moi Avenue in downtown Nairobi, shopping for souvenirs and gifts to bring home.

"Hey, is that Miri and Fritz over there?" My question prompted Eric to search among the many faces in the crowded street to see if he could recognize our friends from Mount Kenya.

"There they are," Eric said, spotting them across the street.

"Miri!" I yelled as we made our way over to them. "Fritz! How are you doing? How was your trip down from Mount Kenya?" The streets were hot and packed with people, so we ducked into a nearby restaurant and ordered cold drinks: two Cokes, a Fanta, and a Sprite. With the risk of unhealthy water ever-present, soft drinks are an unavoidable daily routine in the Third World. As we sipped our drinks, we began exchanging tales of our recent activities.

Miri and Fritz had left Mount Kenya and latched onto a safari to the Masai Mara, the northern extension into Kenya of Tanzania's famous Serengeti Plain. Eric and I told of our journey out from Mount Kenya and our subsequent visit to the Aberdares, a beautiful forested range of hills north of Nairobi. Eric explained that he was returning to Canada that night, and I said I was trying to decide what to do with my remaining time in Africa. Miri and Fritz had 10 days before their scheduled return to Europe and were on their way to Tanzania to try Kilimanjaro.

"We go next day. You come?" Miri asked in his heavy accent.

"Why not?" I said impulsively. "That would be great!" The thought of climbing Kilimanjaro was tempting, and the circumstances might never be better. A plan was born, and suddenly I had a very busy day of organizing for a big climb and seeing Eric off at the airport.

Early on February 1, before the sun changed the cool night air into the oppressive heat of another day in Nairobi, my pack bulging with mountaineering gear, I walked the back streets of the teeming equatorial metropolis to the part of town where the buses for all parts of East Africa departed. Away from the more affluent, tourist-oriented hub of the city, the narrow roads and alleyways were just beginning to come alive.

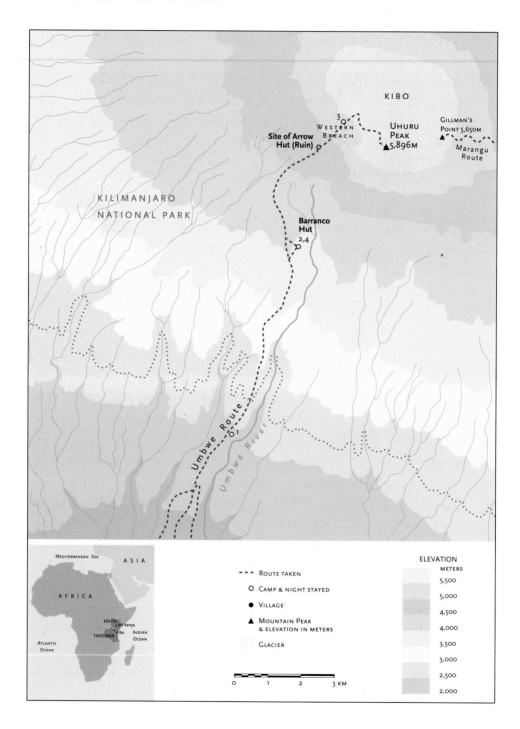

KIBO

3

WESTERN
BREACH

UHURU
PEAK
▲5,896M

GILLMAN'S
POINT 5,650M
▲

Marangu
Route

**Site of Arrow
Hut (Ruin)**

KILIMANJARO
NATIONAL PARK

**Barranco
Hut**
2,4

Umbwe Route

Umbwe River

MEDITERRANEAN SEA

ASIA

AFRICA

KENYA
Mt Kenya
Kibo
TANZANIA
INDIAN
OCEAN

ATLANTIC
OCEAN

ELEVATION

METERS

- - - ROUTE TAKEN

○ CAMP & NIGHT STAYED

● VILLAGE

▲ MOUNTAIN PEAK
& ELEVATION IN METERS

GLACIER

5,500

5,000

4,500

4,000

3,500

3,000

2,500

2,000

0   1   2   3 KM

Storekeepers were unlocking and rolling up the heavy metal shutters that protected their shop windows overnight, while street hawkers pushed wooden carts laden with juicy slices of pineapple and mango. The crowd heading for work was growing, but the sidewalks still contained the flow. The streets were left to the taxis and buses. Soon enough, though, the sidewalks would be unable to handle the pedestrians and the streets would fill with people. Then the assault on the ears would begin, as traffic was forced to a virtual halt and drivers blasted their horns in frustration. The slopes of Kilimanjaro beckoned.

I wove through the throng toward the bus station, arriving to find Fritz and Miri standing by the bus, guarding their packs and ready to go. It was just after 7:00 a.m., and our scheduled departure for Moshi in Tanzania was still 30 minutes away. "Hi, guys," I said, dropping my pack with a weighty thud next to theirs. "The bus looks pretty rough."

"No so bad," said Miri. "Is good, I think."

By 7:35 a.m., after much yelling, horn honking, and what seemed like unnecessary commotion to attract attention, our bus began to wind through the congested streets of Nairobi on its way south to the border. The bus was old, battered, and beaten, driven hard on hard roads. It had obviously been painted a number of times, and perhaps the most recent blend of green, red, and yellow was the current owner's idea of a profitable image, or maybe he had struck a good deal on cheap paint. The driver laid a heavy hand on the horn until we cleared the outskirts of Nairobi, then the conductor punched the latest Zairian disco music into the tape deck. The blare of the repetitive music crackled through the partially blown speakers, and it was only made worse when the volume was boosted to overcome the roar of the vehicle's diesel engine. My head began to ache, while my stomach fought a pitched battle against the greasy one-egg omelet, tea, and white toast with bright pink jam that I had wolfed down for breakfast before getting on the bus. The increasing heat of the day made me sweat, causing my back and legs to stick to the old vinyl seat. The window was jammed and wouldn't open. Thankfully most of the Africans didn't smoke. They were probably too poor. The one exception was the conductor who, wearing the latest imitation American clothing, stood on the steps by the door and puffed away on a foul-smelling cigarette. I watched through the dusty window as the African plains drifted by, consoling myself with the knowledge that I would soon escape.

Reaching the border town of Namanga just before 11:00 a.m., we piled off the hot bus into the more intense heat of the midday sun to be instantly surrounded by hawkers and peddlers, each with his own version of the best product. We had our choice of the cheapest safari, the choicest hotel, the top exchange rate for dollars, the coldest drink, and the finest carvings. The huckstering was relentless, and the continuous need to say no drained us.

We fought our way to the customs and immigration building and lined up for visas to enter Tanzania. The officials were gruff and dirty sweat stained their shirts. The process was tedious for everyone. The line moved slowly. The walls of the concrete building were covered in dull paint that had faded years ago. The roof was corrugated iron and every window – barred, of course – was wide open in a hopeless attempt to cool the waiting rooom. Glumly we filled in our visa applications and currency declaration forms.

The Tanzanian government required all visitors to declare on a form the amount of money they were bringing into the country. To exchange money legally one had to go to a bank. When exchanging dollars for shillings, the bank would record the transaction on your currency declaration form. Then, when you left the country, all the money you spent and the amount remaining in your pocket was supposed to add up. These strict regulations were designed to prevent tourists from trading money on the thriving black market, which offered rates of exchange nearly 10 times greater than any bank. We chose to lie about the amount of cash and traveler's checks we were carrying across the border, leaving open the option of buying shillings on the black market.

Eventually our turn came, and I placed my Canadian passport on the table with my visa application and my currency declaration form. The large man in front of me leafed through my passport, pausing occasionally to inspect previous visas from other countries. He asked no questions. Patience was my only privilege.

The stamp came down with authority on a fresh page in my passport. A quick glance at my currency declaration form and the rubber stamp again descended heavily. When I stepped aside, Miri slapped his passport onto the table and waited. I noticed that his passport was Swiss and stared at it in obvious shock. With mounting trepidation I watched as the officer compared the picture in the passport to Miri; my new friend's unkempt beard, dark, ruffled hair, loose shirt, and blue jeans made quite an untidy package. Miri stood quietly, though, and smiled at the solemn official. I turned and walked away, trying to hide my astonishment. As I left the building, I heard the stamp land.

When we were on the bus again and well on our way to Moshi, I could no longer contain my curiosity. "What's the deal with the Swiss passport? I thought you were from Prague."

"Yes," Miri replied casually, "but people in Czechoslovakia think me in Swiss giving lectures and slides about climbing in Pamir Mountains."

Fritz jumped in and said, "The passport Miri is using belongs to a friend of mine. He would never have been given a visa in Czechoslovakia for traveling to Africa to climb. There are few freedoms there."

"Let me see it," I said, and Miri handed over his passport. "This doesn't look at all like you, Miri. I can't believe you get away with it." The photo on the borrowed passport was of a brown-haired, cleanly shaven face. It was a bold strategy, a huge risk he had taken simply to travel in Africa and climb a couple of mountains.

We arrived in Moshi late in the afternoon. Miri and Fritz immediately set about finding local currency on the black market. A contact was made and we slipped into a narrow shop, brushed past rows of merchandise stacked to the ceiling, and entered a small room at the back that contained a single chair and desk. After a minute, a man stepped in and closed the curtain behind him. We stood there unmoving as the tiny East Indian counted out piles of notes. Fritz gave him two $50 bills, and we walked out of the shop carrying 15,000 in Tanzanian shillings.

We had bought food in Kenya and our equipment was already packed, so rather than spend the night in Moshi, we hired a taxi and left immediately for the tiny village of Umbwe on the southern slopes of Kilimanjaro, arriving at twilight. There was no hotel, no place to stay: the village had virtually no facilities. All of the buildings housed families who worked on the coffee or banana plantations.

"We stay at church," Miri said in his matter-of-fact way. "Is good." I decided this tactic wasn't new to him.

The church was easy to find since it was the largest building in the village. It was dark as we approached the steps to investigate. Everything was quiet and there were no lights on inside. Fritz gave a pull on the big doors at the front, but they were locked. The front deck was covered by a small roof and, after cooking and eating a pot of soup, we laid out our sleeping bags and settled down for the night. I slept well, guarding my pack by using it as a pillow.

The next morning we woke to a combination of sunlight streaming through the trees and the murmur of a growing throng of villagers dressed in clean clothing and wearing hats and polished shoes. It was Sunday. They seemed more surprised than we were but waited patiently while we changed into our clothes, gathered gear, and vacated the front steps of their house of worship.

We packed quickly around the side of the church and set off through the village on the trail toward Kilimanjaro. The rough road led us past the vast coffee and banana plantations that surround Umbwe. It was a beautiful morning, and our first glimpse of Kilimanjaro through the broad green leaves of the banana trees caused us to drop our packs so we could photograph the fabled mountain's snow-capped summit. At that moment an excited group of young boys came rushing up the road toward us. They wanted to work for us as porters on the mountain. Rather than explain that our packs were much too large, I lifted mine onto the back of the largest boy and his knees buckled. It was an object lesson: it would be a few years before they would become porters on Kilimanjaro. They followed us for a short distance before they became bored and escaped into the banana trees, laughing and yelling at one another. We continued walking through the plantation, using the distant summit of Kilimanjaro as our beacon.

The entrance fee for the park was $20 a day. Camping on the mountain was an additional $20 daily. The administration also charged anyone entering the park a contingency rescue fee of $25 and insisted that each party take with it a local guide and pay for his food and supply a wage. The cost for a five-day ascent of the mountain would be at least $250 per person. Miri and Fritz had no intention of paying the fee. Their plan, and mine by default, was to sneak discreetly up the mountain and then back out of the park along the rarely traveled Umbwe Route to the Western Breach. Its description in *Guide to Mounts Kenya and Kilimanjaro*

Fritz loads my pack on the back of an enthusiastic young boy from the village of Umbwe, but this would-be porter still needs a few years before he can manage loads on the mountain.

99

by Iain Allan had attracted us: "An ascent of Kibo by the Umbwe Route is one of the finest non-technical mountaineering expeditions in East Africa. It is a serious route, unsuitable for the solitary or the inexperienced." I was excited about the trip and the thought of climbing Kilimanjaro, and though I wasn't comfortable with this clandestine activity in a country where the justice system could be swift and severe, I found myself unable to resist the adventurous scheme.

We walked quietly up the trail and past a sign that read ENTERING KILIMAN-JARO NATIONAL PARK. Perfect, I thought, we're already into the park and not an official in sight. We continued up the trail, and 200 meters farther on a man in a green uniform emerged from a small building on the right.

"Are you going up the mountain?" he asked bluntly.

It had been predetermined that Miri would be our official spokesman since his accent would be the hardest to understand. "No. One day only. Many taking pictures."

I couldn't believe my ears. We were wearing huge packs with climbing ropes dangling from the top. How could this official possibly conclude that we would be spending only one day in the park?

"Okay, my friends, have a good day." His response was more incredible than Miri's statement, but we set off up the trail and did our best to take his advice.

The jungle that surrounds Kilimanjaro is a dense montane forest. Its canopy virtually prevents any sunlight from reaching the ground and keeps the temperature cool and fresh for walking. We knew we were sharing the forest floor with unseen animals such as the deerlike duiker and the elusive leopard. Above us, Sykes' monkeys swung in the branches and noisy birds cackled.

Routes on the mountain are all long, uphill tracks, but the trail we had chosen, the Umbwe, was a particularly steep, grinding path. We toiled under our heavy loads, sweating with the effort.

"Oh, my God!" I shouted, nearly jumping off the trail. "Look at this!"

I was walking ahead, bent over at the waist, focused only on the few meters in front of me, when I nearly stepped on a half-decayed human corpse lying across the trail. The skin remaining on the skull was dry and pale and clung tightly to the bone, while the rest of the body was little more than a skeleton with pale gray skin hanging loosely off its frame. I sidestepped the remains quickly and felt a cold sensation grip my spine. Fritz moved past carefully without saying anything, while Miri simply dropped his pack.

"What's up?" I asked Miri. "Let's get the hell out of here. This guy looks like someone might have hit him on the head. On top of that, we're in the park illegally. Who knows what might happen in a place like Tanzania?" I tried to envision what tale I might tell the authorities at a local police station. It was an experience I could do without.

"Just some pictures," Miri insisted as he pulled out his large-format camera. He was carrying a load of photographic equipment, and before long he assembled his tripod, fitted his camera with a wide-angle lens, and was set up no more than a meter from the corpse. Meanwhile Fritz and I moved 50 meters up the trail and sat down on our packs, anxious to get going.

After 10 minutes of artistic effort, Miri joined us for a short break. We sipped from our water bottles and discussed what might have happened to the man. Had he been murdered? Had he been brought there to die? Had he been attacked by an animal? We considered several theories. The body had clearly been there for days, possibly a week or more, and I was convinced the man's death had been due to foul play.

"What was that?" Fritz suddenly cried. Then he dropped his voice to a whisper and said, "I thought I heard something."

We sat motionless, listening for an unfamiliar sound in the tranquil jungle. The answer to Fritz's question strode toward us in the shape of a large, muscular black man dressed only in a loincloth. As he moved briskly down the trail, I noticed with alarm that he was carrying a meter-long panga, a machetelike tool used for cutting wood and branches.

Blood dripped from the rusty blade of the big knife, and I closed my eyes and braced myself for the worst, only to hear the man mumble *"Jambo"* as he passed by without breaking stride. With my heart knocking furiously against my chest, it took me a moment to realize the stranger had greeted us in typical Kiswahili fashion. And before I could respond in kind, he was gone.

We started laughing, more with relief than with mirth. Then, seconds later, another man stumbled down the trail. This one carried a medium-sized headless duiker on his shoulders while blood, leaking from the animal's neck, oozed down his left arm.

"Jambo," I said as he lumbered by. Clearly this pair had been poaching in the park and were likely more scared of us than we were of them. Our laughter this time was aimed at ourselves.

The rest of our day was spent moving up the trail under the cover of the jungle. Fritz and I remained continuously in front, stopping often to chat and wait for Miri, who fell farther behind as the day progressed. By 2:00 in the afternoon the daily buildup of clouds on Kilimanjaro threatened rain, so Fritz and I decided to set up a tent for Miri, who finally moaned, "Is no good. I am out from lunch." I chuckled to myself at Miri's mangled attempt to describe in English how miserable he felt.

Darkness came suddenly to the jungle, and I sensed unseen eyes and heard too many strange noises near our camp. My imagination began to conjure up what might be out there in the blackness. I fought the fear of the unknown by envisioning how an African might feel in the "jungles" back home in British Columbia where there were salal thickets, impenetrable slide alder, thorny devil's club, and terrain I felt secure in because of familiarity and knowledge. Fatigue eventually overcame my anxiety and I fell asleep, thinking that fate would determine the jungle's response to our presence. It was a quiet night.

At first light the following morning we continued up the Umbwe trail, passing from jungle into the heather forest that completely surrounds the mountain from 3,000 to 4,000 meters. The sky was clear in the early morning, but by noon the hot air rising off the arid steppes far below had built towering cumulus clouds that engulfed the mountain's summit. Precipitation seemed imminent.

Fritz and I progressed through the last sections of heather forest and into the final zone of plant life that precedes the barren ice and rock of the alpine. Here there was only sturdy tufts of grass, several species of everlastings – delicate lightly colored flowers – and stunning giant lobelias and groundsels. The latter, towering up to 10 meters, are unique to East African mountains. Miri was somewhere behind. He disliked carrying heavy packs and preferred to walk more slowly

*Miri rekindles his energy with some lunch on the arduous approach up the
Umbwe Route on Mount Kilimanjaro.*

and rest more often than we did. By 3:30 p.m., as we hiked along the trail etched into the dry lava scree, a few large raindrops splashed heavily on the rocks. We ran for shelter and ducked under a natural roof formed by hardened lava.

Before we could get our packs off, the sky opened and an intense storm washed across the mountain. Fritz and I sat and waited. We nibbled on chocolate and sipped lemonade, hoping that Miri had managed to find a similar shelter from the torrent. I recoiled deeper into our lair as a loud crack of thunder shook the sky. The severity of the downpour increased suddenly, then the rain switched violently to hail, the small pellets of ice lashing down and bouncing off the rocky ground.

As quickly as the storm began, it ended. Thirty minutes after diving into our rock sanctuary, we stepped out onto the trail, which was covered with a thick coat of hailstones. Having spent the energy they had been accumulating all day, the clouds lost their ominous aspect. A quick glance down the mountain revealed Miri wandering toward us. Fritz and I waved at him, reshouldered our packs, and joined our compatriot on the way to the next campsite.

The Barranco Hut is a rusting tin shelter with a dirt floor and a soot-stained interior located at 3,940 meters on the Umbwe Route. We camped inside, placing our sleeping mats on the piles of dried grass collected by previous visitors. The air tasted of the smoke from countless fires lit by poorly equipped porters attempting to stave off the chill of the night air at high altitude. It had taken 11 long hours on the trail to reach the Barranco Hut, and we all fell asleep shortly after a dinner of pasta and tomato sauce. The sky, full of ivory stars on a perfectly black backdrop, was brilliant, while more than 3,000 meters below us the lights of Moshi twinkled.

The weather patterns were becoming familiar. The morning of February 4 was clear and cold, and Kilimanjaro's western wall loomed in the shadows above. By the middle of most days the convective action of the rising air off the surrounding plains produces clouds and the possibility of precipitation. An early start each day made finding a route on the upper mountain much easier.

We hoped to move up to 4,800 meters and bivouac in the Arrow Hut on the west side of Kilimanjaro. From that point our plan was to climb to the summit the following day and return to the Barranco Hut to sleep. Unfortunately our fatigue from the previous day's efforts contributed to a late start from the Barranco in the morning, and clouds were already beginning to form on the upper mountain.

After two hours the last trace of vegetation was behind us as we climbed into the sterile alpine. Miri was feeling better and managed to set the pace up the long slope of loose scree, while Fritz and I were slowed by the altitude. We passed beneath the impressive Breach Wall of Kilimanjaro. Originally we had discussed the possibility of climbing a technical ice route through that rampart, but the unsettled weather and lack of enthusiasm for what would certainly have been two days on rotten volcanic rock and unpredictable equatorial ice conspired to send us up a route through the much more straightforward Western Breach. I followed Miri's steps in the scree and kept a keen lookout for the Arrow Hut.

By 2:00 p.m. we were in the clouds, and I became seriously concerned that we had bypassed the hut. Visibility was less than 50 meters, and without an altimeter I had no proof of where we were. I yelled to Miri and he sat down on his pack to wait for me.

"I think we're past the hut," I said to him between deep breaths. I had rushed my pace to catch up and was now paying the price as I gasped for what little air was available high on the mountain. "We've been going for five hours. We only had to climb 800 meters. The hut has to be near here."

"Is good. No? We go more up." Miri had no idea where the hut was, and it seemed to me there was little hope of finding it in a whiteout. Fritz was still well behind us, and I didn't have the confidence to say for certain whether the hut was up or down. However, my apprehension was no match for Miri's conviction. We shouldered our packs and continued up into the clouds. Light snow began to fall, and as I followed Miri, I thought about the tent we had left at the Barranco Hut to save weight. My headache from the altitude worsened.

The slope steepened and a narrow rib of rock rising above showed us the way. Miri scrambled up the solid rock and I followed. Each step strengthened my opinion that we were above the Arrow Hut. By 4:00 p.m., after almost seven hours of climbing, I knew for certain that we were too high. I cursed myself for not being more assertive, yet still I followed Miri. Fritz was well below us in the clouds.

Frustrated and worried about the dangers of altitude and our lack of shelter from the weather, I was about to shout ahead when Miri yelled down, "For sure too high! Bivi here. Is good. We stay now."

I dropped my pack onto the small rock ledge that was to be our home for the night and wondered how high we were. I was cold and tired and decided to simply lay out my sleeping bag and crawl inside. Miri started the stove, and by the time Fritz reached our puny bivouac, water for tea was on the boil.

Days and nights are particularly consistent on the equator: 12 hours of daylight, then an abrupt change to night. Dawn comes 12 hours later, the full light of day soon after. Sunset on February 4 was brief but spectacular. We were perched on a tiny shelf high on Kilimanjaro, and for 10 minutes we watched as the sun was absorbed by the billowing sea of clouds. It was a magical performance.

I popped two aspirin for my headache, then curled up to rest. The daytime clouds were already dissipating with the cooling temperatures, and stars now dotted the deep black sky. My sleeping bag wasn't sufficient to combat the cold, and I shivered inside as I searched for elusive warmth, still wondering just how high we were. My guess was 5,200 meters, possibly 5,300. Our plan had been to camp below 5,000 meters. My pounding headache told me I was too high.

I must have dozed, because I awoke with a start, gasping for breath. Panicking, I sat up and looked around. Miri and Fritz were quiet and obviously still asleep. The sky was perfectly clear. Consciously I slowed my respiration and lay down again, but there was no more hope of sleep. I was too cold and was now coughing regularly. A headache throbbed behind my eyeballs. Although I was most likely suffering from a case of Acute Mountain Sickness, a common occurrence at high altitudes, my imagination, spurred by fear, insisted that I was having a recurrence of the pneumonia I had endured six weeks earlier in Mombasa. My creativity flourished for the next few hours as I envisioned high-mountain rescues and the complications stemming from our illegal attempt at climbing Kilimanjaro. With mounting desperation I waited for the 3:00 a.m. alarm to ring.

Every half hour I checked the time, and when the alarm finally sounded, I was anxious to get moving. My headache and cough were uncomfortable, but not enough to make me quit and turn around. We shared a pot of tea, then set off toward the summit of Kilimanjaro by headlamp. After 30 minutes of slow climbing, I was

Fritz contemplates the upper mountain at our high bivouac on the Western Breach of Kilimanjaro. Convective clouds develop on most afternoons as hot air rises off the African plains and cools near the summit of the mountain, providing us with a dramatic backdrop in the evening light.

astonished to pull onto a large, flat expanse and realize that we had reached the crater rim at over 5,700 meters. Our bivouac had been located only 100 meters below, and it was suddenly clear why I was feeling so many symptoms of altitude sickness.

We crossed the plateau, passing beneath massive glaciers sitting on the flat upper reaches of the mountain, and began to ascend the final snow slopes to the top. It was in a similar spot near the summit in 1962 that explorer and author Wilfred Thesiger and two companions encountered a pack of wild dogs. On the plains of Africa these bloodthirsty animals corner a weak member of a herd and dismember it, often devouring its various parts before the whole creature dies. Five dogs stalked Thesiger's party and undoubtedly could have inflicted considerable damage, but they chose not to attack, no doubt judging the assault to be too risky. Their strength is in their survival as a pack, and the loss or injury of one dog near the top of Kilimanjaro would affect them all. Most likely survival for them meant descending to the forest and gambling on an easier victim to hunt and devour.

We saw no animals that day, and just past 8:00 a.m. Miri, Fritz, and I arrived at the gently domed summit of Uhuru Peak, Kiswahili for "freedom." The views in every direction were superb; even Mount Kenya, more than 250 kilometers distant, was visible. Only 16 days earlier Eric and I had climbed that volcano's majestic Ice Window Route. I reflected on what experiences like Mounts Kenya and Kilimanjaro – the hardships and risks associated with mountaineering, the need for a common vision, the physical and mental intensity often required to succeed – meant to me. Beyond the beauty of the environment and the personal satisfaction of accomplishment, sharing the challenge with friends was the most important thing. Friendships formed in such places last a lifetime.

After a group shot near the top, we left the summit, not anxious for any contact with guided groups climbing the mountain from the east on the much more popular Marangu Route. There was no point in risking the success of our clandestine ascent by lingering on the top.

Our descent went without a hitch. By 10:30 a.m. we were back at our high bivouac and ready to pack up. My head was still throbbing, so I was eager to continue down. Lower elevations would vastly improve my condition. The scree slope that was so tedious on the ascent was a blessing as we skidded downward over loose rocks. By late afternoon we were safely in the Barranco Hut, relaxing in the sunshine and happy with our day's effort. My headache had disappeared.

Fritz sat against the wall of the hut, dutifully recording his thoughts in his journal. I lay on my sleeping bag, sipping water and reading Joseph Conrad's *Heart of Darkness*. His shadowy descriptions of the Dark Continent fueled my romantic vision of Africa. As well, the novel's compact size made it a natural for carrying up a big mountain. Miri, in charge of dinner, was creating spaghetti. The simmering sauce was a mixture of cheese, butter, ketchup, and peanuts, while the noodles were being boiled in a chicken soup broth. We would be back in Umbwe the next afternoon, and Miri was providing a new definition for end-of-the-trail stew.

Our evening meal was surprisingly tasty, and by the third pot of tea the sun was setting to the west behind the classic volcanic shape of Mount Meru. We were very tired and sleep came easily.

Our final day on Kilimanjaro dawned beautifully – the fifth consecutive morning of brilliant weather. After breakfast we hoisted the packs, once again full of the ropes, tents, and technical gear we had hauled up for an attempt on the Breach Wall, and began down the steep trail toward Umbwe.

The track through the heather forest led gradually to the jungle, and we moved steadily down, passing familiar landmarks. We came to the spot on the trail where the decaying body had been, but it was gone. Its disappearance only added to the mystery. I was curious to know what had happened but far more anxious to be safely off the mountain without being caught. We pressed on.

In the meantime we devised a plan to avoid the official who had allowed us into the park, ostensibly for a day of photography. Our strategy was to take a fork we had spied on the way up that led somewhere into the banana plantations, a path that we presumed would steer us away from the warden and end up near the village. We pushed forward, confident in our cunning scheme. But when we approached the fork in the trail, we were astounded to see our warden sitting under a large tree, seemingly waiting for us. Standing beside him, leaning on a smoothly polished staff, was a muscular figure who had the appearance of a sturdy fieldhand.

"I talk, okay?" Miri said, taking control as we walked up to the warden.

"My friends," the warden said quietly as he stood and approached us, "you have lied to me. You have spent five days in the park." His companion moved to stand beside him and face Miri. Fritz and I waited silently in the background.

"Is beautiful park. Animals, birds, many, many. We taking pictures, then getting lost." Even after a week with Miri, his statement still astonished me. Lost? For five days? How could he be so brazen, particularly with the ropes and ice axes hanging from our packs? Of course, it was either pay these men a bribe or face the penalty for illegally entering the park. The former option was going to be much less complex; facing discipline from an official authority could cost us plenty of money, or even jail. There was no way of knowing. Even a bribe carried no guarantees, but it was our only reasonable alternative.

"I must report you to the park authorities," the warden insisted adamantly. "You have lied to me."

Miri stood his ground. "Lying? No, no, my friend. Photographs only."

The dialogue between Miri and the warden was painful to listen to. Their exchange was time-consuming due to their poor English and strong accents. By now we knew that the warden could be, and wanted to be, bribed. Had he wanted merely to turn us into the authorities, he would have been waiting with several police or park officials. But that was not the way of East Africa. So we stood at the fork in the trail and waited while the proper protocols and conventions were addressed.

Eventually the warden made his real purpose known. "Prove to me you are my friend and I will tell no one that you were here."

"Some money we have," Miri said slyly, taking the cue. "We give you. Okay? How much money?"

"Twenty dollars, my friend, and you can pass." I couldn't believe my ears at the warden's request. The cost of our trip would have been $750 had we done it by the book, and now we had a chance to escape for a mere $20.

I was overjoyed, ready to pay up and go, when Miri responded with a simple, "Is too much."

Too much! I wanted to scream at him, but I bit my lip. I watched the warden's friend grip his staff and wondered why Miri continued to play the game. Distressed, I waited silently.

Once the contest was engaged, the bartering went quickly. When the negotiations were over, Miri handed the warden four $1 bills. There were smiles all around as we headed down the track to Umbwe. I was flabbergasted.

We arrived in Umbwe to find that, due to fuel shortages, there was only one bus to Moshi each day and it left in the morning. After nine hours on the trail, we had no interest in walking the 30 kilometers to Moshi, particularly at night, so we wandered over to the church. This time we were met by the mission priest. Unbelievably he introduced himself as Father Everest and graciously showed us a small space in the old church where we could safely spend the night. It would have been complimentary to describe the room he offered as rustic, but it was much less conspicuous than the front steps. We slept peacefully.

The bus to Moshi on February 7 was canceled due to lack of diesel fuel, a common occurrence in Tanzania. We were contemplating walking the long road when we heard a rumor that a truck was going to make the trip instead of the bus. The truck wasn't difficult to find. There was a frantic commotion just around the corner as it was swamped by locals trying to get a ride to Moshi.

We pushed our way through the mob and lifted our packs onto the bed of the truck. It was a beat-up old vehicle that sputtered diesel fumes and appeared to be embarking on its final journey. I thought of how much nicer the vehicles in the junkyards at home looked and refused to climb on board, preferring instead to stand on the rear tailgate. I was prepared to leap at any moment should the truck fall apart under the pressure of its bulging load.

The box of the truck was about seven meters long by three meters wide. Estimating how many people were on the vehicle from my vantage point wasn't easy, and I lost count several times due to bumps in the road and tight corners, but there were at least 100 people on board, many of them children. I shuddered to think what would happen if the truck suddenly blew a tire and rolled. In North America such an accident would be a tragedy that would sweep the nation and dominate headlines for weeks. In Umbwe, a tiny village on the slopes of Kilimanjaro in Tanzania, the tragedy would be equally great, but the world would probably never hear about it.

Somehow we made it to Moshi, and the driver collected 50 shillings per person, about 30 cents on the black market. That would be enough money to fill the tank and pay the bribe to get the diesel pumps working. Fritz, Miri, and I escaped into town to find a hotel with a shower and a restaurant for a satisfying meal and the pleasure of a cool African beer – Tuskers from Kenya – in the shadow of Kilimanjaro. We paid for those luxuries using money exchanged on the black market. I couldn't bear the thought of crossing the border the following day without a single stamp on my currency declaration form, so I changed $40 at the bank.

The next day, after a relaxing night in a bed, we set off on the daily bus to Nairobi. We had managed to climb Kilimanjaro covertly, and our stay in Tanzania had been incredibly inexpensive. I was now concerned about the border crossing, wondering how we could possibly convince any immigration officer that the three of us had spent only $40 in eight days in Tanzania. I was beginning to feel like someone who worried too much, but I was so unaccustomed to Miri's blatant disregard for authority that it took some getting used to. I thought about Miri traveling on a false passport and realized my concerns were trivial compared to his audacity.

True to form, Miri simply presented his blank currency declaration form at the border and nothing more was said. His passport was never questioned, and the three of us continued on our way to Nairobi without a hitch. When our bus arrived in the capital in the middle of the afternoon, we were once more greeted with blaring horns and crowded streets.

Miri and Fritz were returning to Switzerland that night, and before dark I had to find a place to stay. I still had two and a half weeks in Africa. We stood beside the bus with our packs on our backs and exchanged goodbyes. It was hard to do. We had climbed a mountain together and as a team had dealt with the many difficulties that always surround such an enterprise. The adventure we had shared had made us partners, and friends.

"Is good, Jim. Bye now and climb safe." I waved goodbye and walked away with Miri's words on my mind and a smile on my face.

TWO MONTHS LATER, while skiing in the Alps, I spent a week living in Fritz's apartment in Switzerland. Although he was absent, he had left a note with his landlord that I might be passing through town, and every hospitality was afforded me.

I never saw Miri again, although we exchanged postcards and I managed to arrange some official letters for him to come to Canada from Czechoslovakia. He climbed in the Pamirs, in the Himalayas, and in Patagonia before ending up in Talkeetna, Alaska, where he lived in a rustic place outside town. He loved the wilderness of Alaska and climbed extensively in the remote corners of the state.

In the spring of 1993 Miri completed a first ascent on the isolated summit of Mount St. Elias, then climbed the three giants of the Alaska Range: Denali, Foraker, and Hunter. Later that summer Miroslav Šmíd tragically fell to his death while rope-soloing Lost Arrow Chimney in Yosemite Valley. Although he is gone, his spirit and sense of adventure remain strong in those who shared the mountains with him.

I know it is with me.

DISCOVERING INNER STRENGTH
Rescue in the High Andes

SHE SAT ON A FENCE away from the excitement, her somber gaze strangely inappropriate for her youthful face. The modern bus in which we had arrived was quickly emptied of brightly colored packs bursting with the latest technical mountain climbing equipment, and soon a sizable pile of gear lay in the dirt beside the road. Donkeys brayed loudly as our provisions were heaped on their backs. Men shouted commands in both Spanish and English, creating even more confusion. Throughout this spectacle the girl refused to grant any significance to the commotion. I distanced myself from the turmoil and studied her face through the telephoto lens of my camera, anxious to capture the certain beauty of her smile on film. But all I saw was dignity, and suspicion – of our group, our relative wealth, and our luxury of choice.

It was the middle of the morning on May 31, 1987, and the day was already hot. We were in Cashapampa, a tiny farming village in the highlands of Peru. The local *arriero,* or burro driver, was loading his horses and donkeys with the food and equipment necessary for our two-week trip into the Cordillera Blanca, a range of towering peaks within the massive Andean Mountains that stretch north to south for more than 8,000 kilometers and form the backbone of South America.

Curious workers sauntered out of the surrounding fields, hoes and shovels in hand, offering unsolicited advice to our *arriero* on how best to secure the awkward loads on the backs of obstinate donkeys. Mothers, with toddlers clinging to their peasant clothing, stood beside their mud-brick houses and watched silently. Older children, those bold enough to approach foreigners, advanced cautiously,

115

An afternoon convective storm rises on the icy West Face of Nevado Yerupaja, the highest peak in the Cordillera Huayhuash, Peru.

crying, "*¡Regalo caramelo!*" Their requests for candy prompted, in very average Spanish, a pleasant "*Buenos días*" and a sweet reward.

We were traveling in South America on a tight budget, carefully spending our dollars only on necessary transportation, lodging, and food. In North America we were considered young and adventurous, but certainly not affluent. In Cashapampa we were rich. For these villagers, activities other than work in the fields, family life around the village, or basic education in the schoolhouse were unrealistic dreams. It was difficult not to feel a bit uncomfortable with the huge difference in opportunity between our group and the local people.

As I focused my camera on the young girl, I pondered the accidents of birth that afforded me limitless opportunities while others in places like this all over the world were born in hopeless poverty. I imagined that she might be pondering the same thing.

There were 12 of us on a five-week mountaineering holiday in Peru – all gringos from North America. Our arrival in Cashapampa that morning had brought village activity to a virtual standstill as the inhabitants gathered near our bus at the end of the dusty road and the beginning of the trail into the mountains. Our plan was to take a trip up the Quebrada Santa Cruz, a valley at the northern end of the Cordillera Blanca that contains dramatic and legendary mountaineering objectives. The climbing goals of our team included the steep snow and ice of Alpamayo's Southwest Face and the sweeping rock buttresses on the West Face of Taulliraju.

We had come that morning by bus from the foothills town of Huaráz. There, we had prearranged the bus ride to Cashapampa and the animals to carry our food and equipment up the Quebrada Santa Cruz. Señor Morales, the owner of the outfitting agency, doubled as the bus driver, and we left the hiring and communication with the local *arriero,* Angel, to him. I watched with both curiosity and concern as our gear was dumped on the backs of eight burros while Angel's three horses escaped with light loads.

"Horses are much more valuable than donkeys," explained James Blench, a team member and veteran of a number of climbing expeditions to Peru. "The *arriero* is sparing his precious horses at the expense of the burros."

*Loading burros with food and mountaineering supplies in the tiny village of
Cashapampa before setting off up the Quebrada Santa Cruz.*

We departed Cashapampa at noon. The sky was a flawless blue and the heat of the equatorial sun persistent. The burros strained with their burdens up the steep trail; whenever one of them showed signs of stopping and resting, it immediately felt the sting of Angel's cane. One particularly scrawny burro was clearly suffering from more than its unusually heavy load, and the struggling animal's foul-smelling diarrhea kept us all at a distance.

Trekking with only light day packs, our group took advantage of the leisurely afternoon walk up the Quebrada Santa Cruz to form new friendships and strengthen bonds between old companions. I could see my brother Kevin ahead on the trail. We had climbed together for years, and I relished the idea of another opportunity to share an adventure in the big mountains with him. He was talking

The view up Quebrada Quilquehuanca, an easily accessed alpine valley above the major Peruvian town of Huaráz.

intently with two of my best friends and climbing partners, Michael Down and Matt MacEachern. I found out later they had been discussing early Christian mysticism.

At the front of the pack was Kevin's girlfriend, Vicki Venner. She had grown up in Ontario and this would be her first trip into the high mountains. Vicki was walking with a skiing and climbing buddy of mine, Peter Mair, and his girlfriend, Liz Wooten. Their pace was typically brisk. I was in the middle of the group, near the train of burros and horses, catching up on news and ideas with James Blench, Dave Stark, and Rob Rohn. Our chat revolved around mountain guiding. We debated the value of certification in guiding and to what degree the attainment of accreditation ensures qualification. The four of us were all guides who were developing personal philosophies about our profession; the conversation was characteristically intense and no firm resolutions were reached.

At the back of the group were Barry Blanchard and his brother Steve. Barry, one of Canada's top alpinists, was building his career by actively seeking out difficult routes on major summits around the world. Not a climber, Steve was a young man who had clashed with the law and was distracted by life in the city. Barry was hoping a journey to the Third World and a challenging trek into the high alpine would help his brother to develop new insights and lifestyle directions. For my part, I was excited and proud to be heading into the mountains on an adventure with such a strong group of climbers and friends.

We set up our first camp near the trail just before dusk. The valley had changed from a steep-sided gorge to a wide and friendly place with a gentle river meandering through alpine meadows. The snowy peaks were still not in sight. We unloaded our burros and feasted on barbecued chicken and fried potatoes bought in Huaráz the night before and packaged in sweaty plastic bags. Unfortunately what had seemed like a good and simple idea for dinner turned out to be a nightmare. James and Vicki vomited soon after going to bed, and the greasy dinner caused upset stomachs among the rest of us. Around the campsite the joking comments were that we now felt a bond with the sick, bony burro that lay on its side, gasping and wheezing, too tired to join its buddies in the grass by the river for dinner. We decided to carry heavier day packs the next day to help the little guy. There was a lot less compassion for Angel.

June 1 brought a perfectly clear dawn. Angel was up early to load his burros because he hoped to reach our base camp by noon and unload so he could complete the return trip down to Cashapampa that night. Our morning trek led us into the heart of the Cordillera Blanca. Tiny lakes glimmered in the sunshine, and icy peaks slowly unveiled their splendor as we turned each new corner.

Before tackling the final hill to our proposed base camp, we rested by the river in lush meadows to allow the burros to catch their breath while we enjoyed a cool drink of water. Angel was anxious to get going, however, and after a short respite he urged his animals on. The exhausted burros needed a good deal of coaxing to make the climb, and Angel's repeated physical urging caused a couple of loads to fall off. I could hear James grumbling something to Barry and Dave about the pathetic quality of our *arriero*.

The spot we chose for our base camp was at the junction of the two main valleys. It was a pleasant, level spot near running water, and Angel let the animals continue up the trail while we discussed where exactly to locate the camp. As soon as we made our decision, the *arriero* let out a whistle, calling his animals back. One of the horses was obviously temperamental. He objected to returning with his load, which consisted of a single duffel bag, and proceeded to buck and kick as if someone had driven spurs into his flanks. Before long he shook the bag loose, booted it, then dragged it several hundred meters until he finally calmed down. Once recovered, the bag was found to contain a good portion of our fresh vegetables for base camp.

James and Vicki, both relatively fluent in Spanish, blistered Angel for his unprofessional handling of the horses and burros. I was impressed by the flow of words and marveled at how quickly and fluidly ideas can be expressed in a Romance language. As I walked away from the discussion, two thoughts came to mind: Angel's tip, already in deep trouble, wasn't going to improve, and the rebellious horse had essentially made guacamole out of our large bag of avocados, which gave me a pretty good idea of what lunch would be.

Angel left with his animals and we set up camp near the river. The site we had planned for our main camp was at the junction of the Quebradas Santa Cruz and Arhuaycocha. To the east rose Taulliraju while to the north, above the Quebrada

Arhuaycocha, towered Alpamayo; the intersection of the two valleys seemed to be the best spot to camp since it allowed equal access to both of our primary objectives. James, Barry, and I went up the valley to get a closer view of the impressive West Face of Taulliraju, while the others spent the afternoon preparing their climbing gear for use during the next few days. Over dinner we discussed our plans.

James and Barry would leave the following day to attempt a difficult climb on Taulliraju, Steve would stay in base camp to safeguard our equipment and try his luck at fishing, and the rest of us, nine in total, would leave in the morning and spend two days to reach the high col between Quitaraju and Alpamayo. From there we would attempt routes on both peaks. We slept that night in the cool air at 4,000 meters, with a bright three-quarter moon and countless distant stars as the only blemishes in the jet-black sky.

The steep and technically difficult West Face of Taulliraju at the head of the Quebrada Santa Cruz.

June 2 was a long, tedious day, the kind that is necessary on most mountain trips but is usually soon forgotten, lost somewhere in the deep recesses of the brain as a bad memory. The approach up Quebrada Arhuaycocha had typical characteristics: cinched hip belts supporting massive packs, a tiresome gravel path winding steeply through jumbled boulders, high-altitude headaches, and the throbbing pain of unseasoned muscles. Michael, who had attempted Alpamayo years before, dubbed the steep terrain at the head of the Arhuaycocha the "Valley of Death." The title seemed a bit dramatic initially, but after our long day's struggle across its loose glacial moraine the name stuck.

Late in the afternoon we finally camped at the toe of the glacier at 4,900 meters, all of us feeling unacclimatized and worn out. The sun was still setting on the surrounding peaks, highlighting with a soft pink glow the amazing snow features common in the Andes, but our fatigue drove us to our sleeping bags despite the impressive display. We knew the following day would bring more hard work under painfully heavy loads.

In the morning everyone stayed in their tents until the sun came over the ridge tops and bathed our camp in its warmth. The weather was once again brilliant. I had now been in Peru for two weeks and had yet to see anything more than the occasional show of billowy white fair-weather cumulus clouds dotting the blue sky. After breakfast we set off across the glacier toward the col in rope teams of three.

The lower glacier was relatively gentle and the going was easy. The final climb up to the col steepened considerably, and that, combined with the altitude of 5,400 meters and the loads on our backs, made the last steps into camp a real struggle. Our camp at the col was established on a flat glacial bench at 5,600 meters. Everyone dropped their burdens with a thud, thankful that from here on our packs would be significantly lighter. There was already a small tent at the col. Two climbers, a Swiss and an Austrian, were camped and preparing for an ascent of Alpamayo the following day.

We had gained altitude rapidly. Discussion centered around whether the next day, June 4, should be a rest day for acclimatization or if an attempt should be made on Quitaraju. Alpamayo was the primary objective. The Southwest Face

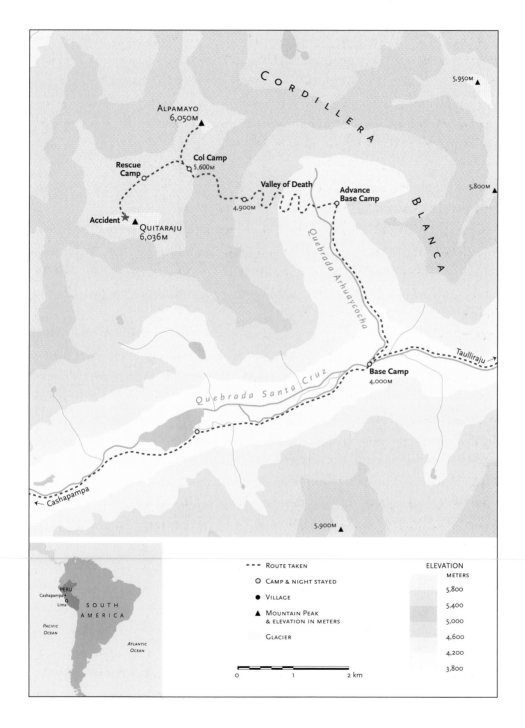

C O R D I L L E R A

B L A N C A

5,950M ▲

ALPAMAYO
6,050M ▲

Col Camp
5,600M

Rescue
Camp

5,800M ▲

Valley of Death

Advance
Base Camp

4,900M

Accident ★ ▲ QUITARAJU
6,036M

Quebrada Arhuaycocha

Taulliraju →

Base Camp
4,000M

Quebrada Santa Cruz

← Cashapampa

5,900M ▲

PERU
Cashapampa
Lima

SOUTH
AMERICA

PACIFIC
OCEAN

ATLANTIC
OCEAN

- - - ROUTE TAKEN

○ CAMP & NIGHT STAYED

● VILLAGE

▲ MOUNTAIN PEAK
& ELEVATION IN METERS

GLACIER

ELEVATION
METERS

5,800

5,400

5,000

4,600

4,200

3,800

0   1   2 km

rose in a sheer pyramid above our camp, and the fantastic snow flutings that dropped abruptly from its summit created a forbidding look. Clearly we wouldn't be ready to climb it until we were thoroughly used to the altitude. The lower angled terrain on Quitaraju made it an obvious choice for a warm-up climb.

Our camp faced northwest, the wrong aspect to catch the early sun, and the morning of June 4 was a cold and shadowy -12 degrees Celsius. Everyone was sluggish. Several had headaches. By the time I was up to take in the morning vista, the two Europeans were already climbing the face of Alpamayo. Over hot tea at breakfast we discussed what each of us would do for the day.

"I'd like to climb Quitaraju," Rob said. "It looks easy enough and would acclimatize us for the route on Alpamayo."

Dave, looking tired and pale, was stuffing his sleeping bag. "I had a terrible night. I spent most of it going to the bathroom. I'm going to base camp and try to get healthy. I'll only get worse up here."

I felt sorry for Dave. Having a case of diarrhea in the Third World is bad enough; having it in the high alpine is really nasty.

"I'm up for a shot at Quitaraju, Rob," Matt threw out from his tent as he laced his boots. "How long do you think it'll take?"

"Four or five hours, I imagine," Peter said, stepping into the conversation from the tent he was sharing with Liz. "I'm in, but Lizzy is staying here."

Michael, Kevin, and Vicki all decided to remain in camp and give their bodies a day of rest and acclimatization. I was torn. I wanted to climb Quitaraju, and three of my best friends were on their way. I had a slight headache and felt a bit queasy but judged I could probably make the ascent, so I tied up my boots and began to get ready.

The route looked like a long snow climb, nothing too serious, but because of my headache I was still unsure if climbing Quitaraju was the right decision. While I was doing up the last buckle on my harness I had a change of heart. "I think I'll stay and hang out today, guys. I just don't feel so great. Are you all right without me?"

Rob was feeling fit and typically enthusiastic. "You bet, Jim. We'll be back this afternoon and give Alpamayo a shot tomorrow. Rest up."

*Matt takes the final steps to the col camp at 5,600 meters
beneath the Southwest Face of Alpamayo.*

"Be safe, guys. We'll have a brew ready when you get back." It was just past 8:30 a.m. as I ducked back into my tent and fell asleep while Matt, Peter, and Rob dropped down the snow ramp below camp and crossed the icefield toward the Northwest Ridge of Quitaraju.

Two hours later I sleepily poked my head out of the tent and heard Kevin and Michael talking in concerned voices.

"That was a huge slide." Michael's matter-of-fact statement cleared my head immediately.

"I hope those guys weren't anywhere near there," Kevin said, expressing what Michael and Vicki were thinking as they watched the dust settle on Quitaraju's Northeast Face.

"I doubt it," Michael said. "They disappeared around the corner 45 minutes ago. I think I'll call them just the same, though." He let go with a loud yodel that carried across the silent mountain landscape. Faint replies gave us mixed feelings. We had thought they were already past the corner, but their response meant they were nearer to the avalanche than we had hoped. Michael let loose with another whoop. Again there was a faint reply, then a louder response from the climbers on Alpamayo. They had reached the summit and must have thought we were yelling encouragement.

Then we heard it again – a feeble response from a few kilometers away. We stood there pondering our next move when a lone figure appeared in the far distance, a tiny black dot on the vast glacial landscape. More faint calls ensued.

"Why do they keep yelling?" Michael asked, thinking out loud. There was a brief pause as the questions in our minds built momentum toward a decision. Finally Michael voiced it. "Let's go."

Kevin and Michael began lacing their boots. They would take basic first-aid supplies and some warm clothes and move quickly across the glacier to get more details. Liz, Vicki, and I would follow with additional equipment: sleeping bag and pads, tent, stove, and extra first aid. My imagination kicked into overdrive as I put on my harness and crampons, and images of what might have happened flashed through my mind.

Matt, Rob, and Peter shouldered their light packs and descended from the col to the flat icefield that led to Quitaraju. It felt good to get out of the shade and into the warm sun, and they stopped to put on sunscreen and glasses. Discovering a track pounded out a week earlier by Italian climbers, they made good time across the flats before beginning the slow upward climb. After an hour and 45 minutes, they paused for a much-needed drink. They were already almost halfway up the face and moving quickly. The route ahead looked relatively easy; in two hours they would be on their first Andean summit.

Their track contoured up the face, avoiding crevasses and snaking past the remains of an ancient icefall – huge blocks of glacial ice hidden under the winter snow. They continued upward, mesmerized by the rhythm of their steady breathing at over 5,800 meters.

Suddenly an explosion of snow and ice hurtled toward them.

"Avalanche!" Rob screamed.

"Run!" Peter shouted in desperation, wishing there was somewhere to go, somewhere to hide from the ice blocks bearing down on them. Impact was imminent.

"Which way?" Matt yelled in the second they had to think about ways to alter their fate. The rope that protected them from crevasses now limited their ability to move independently.

Everything happened in an instant. There was nothing they could have done.

Masses of ice, some the size of refrigerators, pounded down around them. Peter was hit on the head and knocked out at once. Rob sensed a sharp blow on his back, then felt the bone in his leg give way. He collapsed on the snow as the avalanche thundered by. Repeatedly hit by blocks of ice, Matt suffered three blows to his head before he had a chance to pull his arms up for protection. He waited to die.

Just as quickly as the avalanche began, it ended and was followed by silence.

Matt was conscious, and surprised to be alive. His feet were uphill, with the rope wrapped neatly around his ankles. He saw Rob directly across the slope, lying among the debris of ice and snow.

"Rob!" he cried. "Rob, are you okay?"

"My leg's totally trashed!" Rob croaked in response.

Matt's mind was overwhelmed by the desperate state of their predicament. As he worked the tangle of rope from his feet, he began to regain his composure. His extensive first-aid training came instinctively to the surface and he started to assess the situation. Rob was alive, hurt but breathing. But where was Peter? He scanned the debris and located him behind a block of ice, face up and motionless.

Matt stood and felt a burning pain race up his leg and into his hip. He stumbled and gasped, then grabbed his ice ax for support and clawed the 20 meters to Peter. He had to get to him. "Peter, can you hear me?"

"We're dead. We're dying. We're dead," Peter mumbled groggily.

"Peter, it's Matt. We're okay. You've been hit on the head by ice. Can you take a deep breath?"

To Matt's relief, Peter responded with a heavy gulp of air, and slowly he found his way back to consciousness. As he came around, Matt began to solicit his help. "Peter, you've been hit on the head. We've been in an avalanche. I need your help. Rob's hurt. I think his leg might be broken. We've got to get out of here."

It was too much, too quickly, for Peter. He was confused, sick to his stomach, and the gash in his head throbbed. Cautiously he ran his fingers behind his left ear and felt a sticky mat of blood and hair. At the same time he sensed the heat of the sun on his skin and could smell the sweet scent of sunscreen. Basic stuff. Matt's instructions and descriptions were too perplexing. Bit by bit, though, Peter's strength began to reemerge. "What should we do, Matt?"

"I'll belay you out to the edge. Tell me what it's like over there."

Peter wobbled to the edge of a huge ice cliff. "It . . . it looks okay. I can see the camp at the col. Should we yell for help?" Peter was still feeling confused, but the logic of his idea was clear.

Matt and Peter screamed for help, hoping someone at the col camp would hear. Then Matt tied Peter off to his ice ax, unfastened himself from the rope, *and stumbled over to Rob. Looking carefully at Rob's left leg, Matt realized that his friend had been right: it was totally trashed. Matt moved him gently to help him take off his pack, causing him to shriek, "Aaggh! My back!"*

"Oh, man! Sorry, Rob. Let's just move slowly. Can you wiggle your toes and fingers?"

"I . . . I think so. I hope it's all right. It's just really sore."

Matt responded with care and attention to Rob's injuries. Unconsciously he turned and gazed up at the skyline to where the avalanche had originated. An hour earlier the ice cliffs had looked like dormant sculptures. Now they were an impending menace.

Rob followed Matt's glance. "God, please don't let another one come down on us."

Matt did what he could to treat Rob: warm clothes for shock, insulation from the snow, rigid support for the broken leg. The back would have to wait. "I'm going to check on Peter, Rob. How do you feel?"

"I'm okay. Thanks. Let me know how Peter is." With those words Rob began the tireless display of composure and gratitude that would survive several days of being bumped, jostled, and battered over rugged mountainous terrain.

Matt returned to Peter to find him sitting in the snow and still dazed. They tried yelling together, a frantic call for help. Their efforts resulted in movement at the col camp – little "ants" scurrying among the tents. And they thought they heard a faint sound that might be a reply. They shouted again.

Carefully Matt organized Peter with warm clothes and sunglasses, then lowered him so that he was shielded behind a large block of fallen ice. It was all Matt could think to do. He wanted to protect Peter from the threat of another icefall.

Returning to Rob's position, Matt gave his injured comrade two tablets of Tylenol #3 and an intramuscular dose of 10 milligrams of morphine from the first-aid kit. Twenty minutes later he repositioned Rob's leg and tightened the splint. Then he noticed two tiny figures climbing up the glacier below, moving quickly. Three more were well behind, traveling across the flats . . .

MICHAEL AND KEVIN were far ahead of us on the glacier when Vicki, Liz, and I left camp. By then we were sure that something was wrong. But what? Our answer came soon enough. As we reached the flat glacier and began moving toward Quitaraju, we saw someone go to the edge of a huge ice cliff and yell information down to Kevin and Michael. The words were Matt's: "Icefall. Rob's back. Peter's head. Matt okay. Need help."

All I could hear was "Rob's dead."

My body went limp. My knees wobbled. My mind reeled in disbelief. Rob dead? How? We had shared so many wonderful times; some had been difficult and dangerous, others exhilarating and beautiful. Alternating waves of logic and emotion crashed through my brain. The rational thoughts told me to move quickly and get to the accident site so I could help my friends. Then my throat seized up and my breathing became difficult as I allowed my feelings of loss to paralyze my ability to move forward. Quickly, though, I chased the useless emotions from my mind, gained control, and returned to the duty at hand. However, as we crossed the glacier, grief still threatened to overwhelm me.

Suddenly the rope went taut and I spun around to see Liz on the snow gasping for air. Distracted by the anguish I was feeling, my pace had quickened. Liz, struggling to keep up and fighting her anxiety over Peter's grave predicament, had collapsed. After several minutes she recovered but was in no condition to continue. I took what gear I could and left Vicki and Liz to care for each other while I continued.

I cursed my inability to move faster. Minutes passed. As I toiled up the final steep slope to the accident site, frustrated by my sluggish pace and ridiculously heavy load, I was grateful to see Kevin descending to give me a hand.

"Everyone's alive, Jim! Rob's leg is broken and his back is banged up. Peter's got a nasty cut in his head. Matt's hurt, but he's been incredible. He's held everything together. Give me the pack. That thing's huge." There was plenty on Kevin's mind and he was rambling.

"Great work, Kev," I said, helping him shoulder the load. I couldn't believe that Rob was alive. Relief brought tears to my eyes. "Thanks."

"Matt's already given Rob a shot of morphine, but we've got to get them out of here. Wait till you see the size of those hunks of ice." Kevin climbed quickly up the hill, even carrying the heavy pack, while I caught my breath and tried to think of a plan.

There was no point in waiting for any other rescue help. That option didn't exist in Peru. The threatening ice above made us even more aware of the need to leave as soon as possible.

With our limited rescue supplies we did what we could to support Rob's injuries. He had definitely damaged his back, and we stabilized it by sliding him carefully on two Thermarests with several pack stays crossed between. I prayed that the back injury wasn't too serious. The splint we had arranged for his 196-centimeter, 86-kilogram frame was only borderline. The next step was to wrap him in a sleeping bag. Then we slipped the whole package inside a small tent, lacing it tightly like a shoe. The resulting tension stiffened the improvised brace, allowing us to slide Rob down the steep face, one rope length at a time.

Peter squints at the glare off the glacier in the rescue camp at 5,400 meters. The swelling from the cuts on his head and face subsided and it was time for him to descend to the valley.

Matt and Peter, now fit enough to get themselves down, led the way and removed icy blocks of avalanche rubble to clear a path for the descent. Michael and Kevin worked the front of Rob's package while I managed the anchors and the ropes at the back.

Given the extent of the injuries, the altitude, and the remote location, the descent went relatively well. We had one major obstacle on the way down – a large bergschrund, or gap, in the ice, which separated the upper face from the lower slopes. We had used gravity to aid the descent, sliding Rob directly down from the accident site. Now we would have to negotiate a five-meter overhanging drop.

We spent several minutes discussing strategy. With our roles defined, Kevin, Michael, and Matt rappelled over the edge and cleared a trough for Rob to follow. Peter and I prepared an anchor and tied our patient off while everything else was made ready. I looked up from my efforts and spied Vicki and Liz crossing the

*Lowering Rob's prone body from the accident site to the flat
glacial bench at 5,400 meters.*

glacier, returning to the col camp. I filed that information away for later and returned to the task at hand.

"Are you guys ready down there?" I asked, wanting to make sure everyone was organized. Any mistakes on this move and Rob's injuries could get worse.

"Ready, Jim," Kevin said from below. "Lower any time."

Peter began easing out rope while I guided Rob over the lip. His feet were stuck out over the edge when, abruptly, the steady movement stopped.

"Don't stop now, Peter! Keep it moving!" I yelled, wondering if it had been a mistake to let Peter manage the ropes in his muddled state.

"It won't go," Peter replied apologetically.

I surveyed our system quickly and realized right away that I had forgotten to undo the backup line we had used to secure Rob while we prepared to lower him. Now it was taut. Angry with myself, I strained to pull our patient back up while Peter released the knot.

"Sorry, Peter. Have you got that knot? Great." This time I was apologetic. "Okay, guys, let's try again. Here he comes."

Rob hung in midair for several anxious seconds until he was guided by half a dozen hands to a flat spot on the downhill side of the bergschrund.

"How was it, Rob?" Kevin asked, afraid that we had aggravated his injuries.

"It felt okay. Good work. Thanks." Even through his morphine haze, Rob responded characteristically. Below the bergschrund the remaining slopes were easily managed by guiding and hauling our invalid friend down the fall line.

Vicki and Liz were just arriving at the col camp as our tired and shattered group came to a halt at the low point on the glacier. The time was 5:00 p.m., and it would be impossible to haul Rob up to the col before dark. There was no option; we would be forced to camp on the glacier.

"Bring everything down here!" Kevin yelled up to Vicki and Liz, but the distance smothered his words. His prompt was unnecessary, they already knew what was needed: they began stuffing sleeping bags and collapsing tents.

It was essential that we recruit more help. We decided that Michael and Kevin should leave at once and try to reach our base camp in Quebrada Santa Cruz that night. Less than two hours of light remained, so we exchanged brief goodbyes and they hurried away. My role, because of my first-aid experience, was to stay with the injured climbers.

Kevin and Michael reached the col in half an hour. For the first time Vicki and Liz were made aware of what had happened, and both were relieved to know that everyone was alive. From their distant perspective they had seen only a body being lowered in a bag. Kevin and Michael had a quick snack and descended into the Quebrada Arhuaycocha in dwindling daylight. By 7:30 p.m. it was completely dark. They continued down by headlamp, bumping their way through the boulders below the glacier. The trail through Michael's Valley of Death was impossible to find, so they relied on instinct. Three hours later, still stumbling toward the Quebrada Santa Cruz, they saw four headlamps coming their way.

James and Barry had been climbing steadily on an extremely difficult route on the West Face of Taulliraju when, at about 10:30 a.m., they "just got a feeling" and decided to retreat. Astonishingly their decision to abandon the route happened within 10 minutes of the avalanche on Quitaraju, an event they had no way of knowing about. They did several rappels to get off their climb and continued back to base camp, reaching it in the late afternoon. Meanwhile the two Europeans on Alpamayo saw our rescue and raced down to the Quebrada Santa Cruz to get help. They arrived in our base camp five minutes after James and Barry and recounted a story of an avalanche and several hurt climbers on Quitaraju. James, Barry, Dave, and Steve knew right away they were in for a long night.

The meeting on the trail was an encounter that brought relief to both parties. One was armed with information, the other with fresh energy. The plan was revised.

It was decided to send Michael and Dave to Huaráz at dawn. They left immediately for base camp by headlamp. Meanwhile James, Barry, Steve, and Kevin bivouacked under the stars, proposing to climb to the col at first light. James brewed tea and cocoa until everyone was content. The long, physical hours of the day made sleep easy.

The tent we had used so effectively to drag Rob down the face became his shelter with no additional jostling of his leg or back. I marveled at how well it all worked, almost as if it had been our design. To execute the rescue we had to rely mostly on our ability and experience, but as the tent popped up around Rob with the simple insertion of the supporting poles, I knew that any such refined trick was solely a product of good fortune.

The shift from day to night began with the disappearance of the sun behind the mountain ridges. The temperature dropped rapidly. A steady breeze forced Peter, Matt, and me to the lee of Rob's tent while we waited for Vicki and Liz to arrive. Matt and Peter were exhausted. It was essential that we get them inside a tent and into warm sleeping bags.

By nightfall there was still no sign of Vicki and Liz. Matt and Peter crawled inside the tiny tent with Rob, while I pulled Rob's large insulated suit from his day pack and slipped it on over my light clothing. On my body the knee patches were closer to my ankles, but the warmth was welcome. Then, gritting my teeth, I set out into the cold wind toward the col by headlamp. Twenty minutes later I found Vicki and Liz using ropes to manipulate three large packs of equipment and food down the steep snow ramp from the col. We hugged, shouldered the loads, and returned quickly to our injured friends.

Camp was swiftly established. Tents went up and Matt and Peter crawled inside sleeping bags for a much-deserved rest. Matt gave Rob our last shot of morphine; we still had to remove his plastic double boot. That would mean disassembling the splint Matt had used to stabilize the fracture. It would be an agonizing process. We knew Rob had circulation in his toes – he could still wiggle them – but it was important that we completely assess his injury now that the circumstances were a bit less desperate. But how we would get Rob out of that remote place was still the overwhelming question. We were relying on our friends for an answer. Our role was to manage the current situation.

While we waited for the morphine to take effect, Vicki and Liz made hot drinks on the stove. I shaved a patch of Peter's scalp to clean and close the vicious gash in the back of his head. The edges of the deep cut were dried up and ragged. Briefly I considered closing it with sutures from the first-aid kit, but my experience with such techniques was limited to practice attempts on an orange rind in a warm classsroom. So I did my best to tack the wound together with Steri-Strips and covered it with gauze and tape. Peter would have to live with the scar tissue.

It was at this point that we realized Matt had sore eyes. He had carefully stowed his snow-covered sunglasses away inside his pack after the avalanche while diligently treating Peter and Rob at the accident site. It was the first time he had mentioned any problem; we had all failed to notice that he had spent the entire afternoon without his sunglasses.

Rob was groggy as Vicki and I crawled into his cramped tent. The night's first stars blinked in the sky as we prepared to do our first aid by headlamp.

"Okay, Rob, we're going to remove the boot now. Vicki, you stabilize the fracture while I remove the boot." I was crowded into the back of the small tent as Vicki slid her hands down Rob's leg to support the broken ends and I undid the ties that held the splint. "We can't stop, Vicki. This is going to hurt him, but we have to keep going. Ready?"

"Ready."

As I removed the boot, I could see right away that the bone ends were badly displaced. The fractured tibia looked like the center pole of a circus tent: the distal end was threatening to push through the taut skin. As I straightened Rob's leg and applied traction, he screamed. His cries of anguish disappeared into the cold air of the high Andes. No one else heard his screams; we were alone. With the splint on, Rob drifted back into a morphine haze.

Michael and Dave moved quickly down the trail to Cashapampa before dawn on June 5. At the same time James, Kevin, Barry, and Steve ate oatmeal by headlamp, then set off for the col. Rob woke up as the sunlight hit his tent. I was curled uncomfortably around his feet, tired but grateful that the night had passed without further incident. That same moment the brightness of the day assaulted Matt's eyes. He was snow-blind. Each time he opened his eyes the light stabbed like a knife. Our only possible treatment consisted of cold compresses, painkillers, and complete darkness. Peter woke with a stiff neck and a sore head but much more himself than the previous day.

Vicki and I climbed back to the col after breakfast to gather more food and leave a note for whoever might be coming up to help. We had no way of knowing what plans had unfolded below. We trudged back to the rescue camp in the late morning, with the intense heat of the day sucking away the last reserves of our energy. Lethargy dominated the rescue camp.

"Anyone order Chinese food?" are Barry's first words as he, Kevin, and James
arrive in the rescue camp with the first wave of support.

137

We snacked on crackers and cheese for lunch. Shelter from the sun became our priority. I was melting snow for water when I looked up toward the col and saw a rope team of three people coming our way. As they neared, I recognized Kevin's distinct side-to-side gait. Help had arrived. The downcast atmosphere in camp shifted immediately. Vicki, Liz, and Peter scrambled out of their tents to greet the approaching climbers.

"Somebody order Chinese food?" Barry, the leader of the rope team, cracked. His bizarre question was completely unexpected, but its impact was significant. It was as if someone had opened a window and let fresh air into a dank, dusty room. Instantly we were completely recharged by Barry's buoyant energy. Kevin hugged Vicki. James slapped me on the back. Smiles lit up tired faces, and for a moment we stopped worrying about the problems ahead. For the first time we could see that the situation was manageable.

We shared a lively exchange of stories and news. Steve, who had started out with the three of them at dawn, had found it too difficult to keep up and had returned to base camp. Lunch was served again – we were ravenous – and a plan was formulated.

James and Barry were fresh and seemed the logical people to stay at the rescue camp with Rob and Matt. Rob would need either a helicopter evacuation or a proper rescue litter with plenty of people to help get him out of the mountains. Matt's eyes were now swollen painfully shut, which would leave him paralyzed in camp for at least another day. The rest of us, including Peter who was sore but mobile, would climb over the col and descend to the Quebrada Arhuaycocha and join Steve at base camp. This would help preserve the remaining supplies at the rescue camp. We left at 3:00 p.m.

It took a long hour to climb to the col where we met four Yugoslavian climbers and two Americans. Both teams were there to attempt Alpamayo. After hearing our tale, all volunteered to help with the rescue. We graciously accepted their offer but couldn't linger; the remaining daylight was ebbing quickly. Using headlamps through the final portion of the rocky moraine, we reached the valley bottom an hour after dark. Kevin located the same bivouac site he had shared with James, Barry, and Steve the night before. Soup and rice were cooked for dinner, then we all fell into a deep sleep.

In the meantime Michael and Dave had spent the day jogging to Cashapampa where they arranged a ride to Huaráz, arriving there at 6:00 p.m. Their search for help began at the Andino Hotel. The owner, Mario, was Swiss and had lived in Peru for many years. His understanding of both the Peruvian system and Western expectations made him invaluable as an organizer of the rescue effort from the outside.

Once the story had been told and what resources that might be needed were explained, Mario took over. Michael and Dave collapsed on the couch in the lobby and were given dinner. The phone to Lima was buzzing, but the hurdles were substantial. The only helicopters in Peru were operated by the military. Mario was told there were no private rescues. No exceptions.

Mario's pleading over the phone was overheard by one of the hotel guests, an influential Peruvian visiting Huaráz on business. In response to his questions, Mario explained our predicament, and the unknown businessman suggested that he might call his friend, a general in the air force.

It was a short call and the general agreed that the helicopter could be arranged – just this one time – but he needed $15,000 cash up front to cover all the flying time and any eventualities. None of us had that kind of money, so the Canadian embassy was brought into the mix.

Mario continued to work his magic. He organized the local mountaineering rescue team, Peruvians with experience as high-altitude porters and guides, and found a rigid stretcher somewhere in Huaráz. By midnight Michael and five Peruvians were on a charter vehicle to Cashapampa. Dave caught the night bus to Lima, arriving there eight hours later. His demanding role would be to liaise with the military, explain the situation to the Canadian embassy, and arrange the $15,000 deposit for the helicopter.

Back in the mountains, dawn on June 7 was again clear, and the five of us camping in the Arhuaycocha pampered ourselves with a late start. It was obvious that Peter felt terrible. His injuries had been aggravated by the descent, and although he was clearly sore and tired, he voiced no complaints.

Our immediate goal was to cover the final kilometers to the Quebrada Santa Cruz and base camp. We walked for an hour before sitting down to rest, our last stop before base camp and a proper breakfast. Kevin was the first to notice another group on the other side of the valley moving up into the Arhuaycocha. "Probably more climbers heading for Alpamayo."

"Look," Liz said as we stared across the way. "That burro's carrying something shiny."

I pulled out my binoculars. "I can't be sure, but I think it's a stretcher."

We had trouble believing that any rescue attempt could have already reached this stage. How could Michael and Dave possibly have managed such a rapid organization of people and equipment? There was no sign of our friends with the group, so we decided to continue on to base camp and wait for news there.

As we got to our feet, shouts from the other side of the valley halted us. I went to meet a Peruvian who was running down to the river. He splashed through the water in his sandals to join me and together we climbed back up to the trail. The story slowly unfolded. Michael had gone to base camp and was packing all of our gear in order to move it to the head of the Quebrada Arhuaycocha. He had joined forces with these five Peruvians and had traveled quickly up the Quebrada Santa Cruz, anxious to begin the rescue as soon as possible.

The remainder of the Peruvian team and their burros crossed the river to join us. From their supplies they kindly treated us to a trailside snack of bread, cheese, and sardines. Famished, we wolfed down the offer. Then, somewhat refreshed, we turned and retraced our steps to establish an advance base camp at the bottom of the moraine.

At the rescue camp Matt awoke that morning to blurred but improved vision. His hip was stiff. Sleeping pills continued to help him pass the time until his eyes could function again. Rob felt that his back was getting better, but to ease the throbbing in his leg he practiced meditation and counted on doses of Tylenol #3 every four hours. Both patients were tended to with care by James and Barry: chicken soup, water, light food, and conversation. All four had little choice but to wait.

Our advance base camp soon expanded when four British climbers, with ambitions for Alpamayo, appeared from the Quebrada Santa Cruz. They had met Michael on the trail and had already heard the story of the avalanche and the injured climbers. Generously they offered two VHF radios for our use during the rescue. Communication could be crucial and the radios would be an enormous help. Our resources were expanding rapidly.

The five Peruvians were eager. Their plan was to reach the col that afternoon with the stretcher. We inspected their meager equipment: two of them were wearing homemade sandals and most had only woolen blankets for sleeping. Kevin suggested they use some of our excess gear. Liz's boots fitted one and we distributed assorted ice axes, crampons, clothes, and ropes among them. Once they were ready to go they surprised us all by taking a siesta, curling up in the midday sun and catching up on some of the sleep they had lost from the previous night. I took the opportunity to write a brief note to our friends at the rescue camp, explaining the situation.

Before the Peruvians awoke from their nap, Michael arrived from the old base camp. His story filled the gaps in our information. Moments later, just after 3:00 p.m., the Peruvians woke up and departed for the col. After three hours of steady climbing, they reached the toe of the glacier, about halfway to the col, where they bedded down for the night. Their time estimate to the top had been a bit optimistic, but given the poor quality of their camping equipment, a night at lower elevation at the toe of the glacier, and an early start in the morning, made more sense.

There were seven of us left at the advance base: Kevin, Michael, Vicki, Liz, Steve, Peter, and myself. It was a pleasure picking over the plentiful food supplies for dinner, each of us snacking on whatever appealed at the moment. Before going to sleep we set the alarm for 3:30 a.m., since Kevin, Michael, and I planned to reach the col by 9:00 a.m. I snuggled deeply into my sleeping bag to ward off the cool night air and nodded off immediately.

"I think it might be time to quit climbing mountains," Michael suddenly said, bringing me back from the edge of sleep. We were sharing a tent, and although he was obviously very tired, it was equally obvious he wanted to talk.

"What do you mean?" I asked, knowing full well that his blunt statement was really a request for me to listen to his thoughts. The mountains and climbing had helped shape Michael's identity for the past 10 years. He wouldn't make such a declaration lightly.

"It's just too dangerous. Too many of my friends, too many people I know, have been hurt, or killed. I just think it might be time to stop." He paused for a moment.

"Look at this trip. Three friends chopped down by an icefall. They're lucky to be alive."

"Do you really think stopping is the answer?"

"I don't know. But I think this might be my last big mountain trip." Our tent went silent after Michael's final words.

I drifted into sleep, wondering whether Michael's outlook would change with time. My perspective on this incident was still unclear; I would have to wait until the rescue was over before I analyzed the events.

Thousands of kilometers away in Canada telephones were ringing across the country. Dave had arrived in Lima and managed to reach friends back home and explain our plight. The Canadian embassy in Lima couldn't guarantee the $15,000 that the Peruvian air force demanded for the rescue. For the embassy to stand behind our rescue the necessary funds would first have to be in the hands of the Department of Foreign Affairs in Ottawa. Rob's parents were contacted in Ontario, and our story spread through his hometown of Canmore, Alberta. Eventually Hans Gmoser of Canadian Mountain Holidays, Rob's employer, put up the money. Very quickly after that the ball began to roll. Dave was introduced to various air force personnel and an early-morning flight was arranged. Unknown to us, a local television cameraman would join the pilot, copilot, and Dave in the helicopter to the Quebrada Santa Cruz.

It was cold at 3:30 a.m. on June 7 and the sky was clear. The alarm rang precisely and without mercy. Grudgingly I slipped out of my warm bag and went to Kevin and Vicki's tent. "Kev," I whispered. "Kev, it's time to get up." I tried not to wake Vicki.

"Okay," Kevin answered wearily. "I'll be out in a minute." We were all tired.

He joined me as I rustled through the food pile in search of something for breakfast. "Michael's going to grab another hour of sleep. He's really tired from his trip to Huaráz."

Then it was 4:00 a.m., and Kevin adjusted his headlamp. "It's cold. Let's get going."

Carrying only light loads, we moved rapidly. Despite the darkness, we surprised ourselves by reaching the toe of the glacier by 6:00 a.m. There was a scheduled radio check with Vicki for that time and we welcomed the rest.

"Hello, Vicki. It's Jim. Do you copy?"

"Hi, Jim." Vicki replied, her voice sounding too cheery for such an early hour. "You're loud and clear."

"You're clear, too. How are things?"

"Michael's still in bed. He must be really zonked. Otherwise everything's okay."

"Great. We'll give you a shout again from the col at nine. We can see the Peruvians ahead of us on the glacier. They're almost at the col, so the stretcher is on the way. Talk to you later." We had previously decided to keep the chatter on the radios to a minimum to conserve battery power. The initial check had been a success. Kevin and I stepped into our crampons and roped up for the trip to the top.

At the rescue camp Matt awoke to the sound of Spanish drifting across the glacier. His eyes were red and swollen, but he could see. Minutes later the Peruvian rescuers arrived. James and Barry read my note and decided that Matt should move to the col to meet Kevin and me at 9:00 a.m. An hour later Barry and Matt were roped together and moving slowly across the high icefield.

Kevin and I made it to the col on schedule and chatted with Michael on the radio. He was enjoying toast and tea with the British climbers. After that we started down to the rescue camp. Before long we met Barry and Matt coming up, so we turned around and headed back to the col.

It was 9:30 a.m. There was still no sign of a helicopter, and for the first time during our two weeks in the Andes, clouds began to build in the east. We decided that Matt should continue down to the Arhuaycocha accompanied by Kevin while Barry and I returned to the rescue camp to help prepare Rob for a helicopter evacuation. Kevin gave me the radio and we scheduled our next contact with base camp at 2:00 p.m.

Kevin carried a heavy load back down from the col and Matt limped, so their pace was unhurried. Clouds swirled around them and light snow started to fall. They passed the descent by reliving the previous few days. Then, suddenly, they heard the heavy beat of a helicopter rotor. Through the clouds they spied what looked like a big bird landing in a green meadow in the Quebrada Arhuaycocha. It came to rest near our advance base camp and shut down. When Kevin and Matt reached the moraine, they heard the engines fire up and watched the helicopter lift and disappear around a ridge to the south. Ten minutes later it returned, only to vanish again.

Barry and I reached the rescue camp to find James packing up tents and gear with the Peruvians. Rob was still in his tent.

"How are you doing, Rob?" I asked, knowing he was probably getting tired of answering that question.

"The back's feeling better, but my leg still throbs a lot. Pretty good, though. I wonder what kind of helicopter they're sending in?" Among us Rob was the most familiar with helicopters. He worked every winter as a heli-ski guide.

"I don't know, but this weather isn't going to help." Black clouds were building over the Amazon Basin to the east. "I'm going to give these guys a hand packing up. Talk to you soon." We organized all the gear in packs and prepared Rob for his trip on the metal stretcher.

Just then the distinct sound of a helicopter came around the ridge, and we jumped into action. It was almost noon and clouds had built over the glacier, leaving only a few gaps between them for visibility. We could hear the helicopter distinctly, but the clouds obscured our view.

The radio sparked to life. "Does anybody copy me?"

"This is James. Go ahead."

"Hi, James. It's Dave." Vicki had given him one of the British radios. "I'm in the helicopter with two Peruvian pilots, but the weather doesn't look too good. We're staying above the clouds at 5,500 meters. They don't want to land because it's too risky with this weather." Dave was translating as best he could. "We're going to Huaráz, but we'll be back first thing tomorrow. The pilot wants Rob to be in the valley for pickup."

James mentally calculated the technical hoist up to the col and then the rugged descent to the valley bottom on the other side. "It's already late in the day, Dave. I don't think we'll be able to make it."

"I know, James, but these guys don't want to fly in here again."

"Okay. We'll do what we can." The helicopter was already disappearing from our valley, its thudding beat diminishing to a gentle tick.

Dave's message was very clear, and we set to work. The eight of us – five Peruvians, James, Barry, and I – began to pull Rob toward the col in the stretcher, taking more than two grueling hours to reach it. As we neared our destination, we were grateful to be joined by the four Yugoslavs and two Americans who were camped there. We arrived at the top a little after 2:00 p.m. It was snowing moderately.

The radio call to our advance base was brief. We would do what we could but only expected to reach the toe of the glacier by nightfall. Maybe the pilot could make a pickup at that point if we found a suitable landing spot. If not, we would need as much help as possible at dawn to get over the moraine. With that we began a long afternoon of easing Rob down the glacier.

The first rope length out of the col was the steepest. James was at the top with the leader of the Peruvian rescue team while Barry and I guided the stretcher down the slope. We targeted a flat spot 50 meters away where we could regroup for the next lowering. The terrain was so steep that the downward pressure of Rob's body weight in the stretcher was hard on his leg.

"It's hurting his leg, James!" I yelled up the slope. "Can you go any faster?" The

Lowering Rob down the broken glacier that plunges from the col between Quitaraju and Alpamayo.

145

response was immediate and the stretcher picked up speed.

Three meters from our next station the rope tightened and the stretcher jerked to a stop. Rob groaned in agony. "What the hell's up?" I screamed into the blowing snow. "Keep it moving!"

James cursed at the top of the slope. "The knot's jammed. I'm going to cut it. Can you take the weight?"

Barry and I braced ourselves and prepared to hold the stretcher. "Cut it!" Barry yelled up to James. As we slid Rob down the last part of the steep slope, I concentrated on simply holding on, desperately trying to ignore his muffled sobs.

With Rob finally in a horizontal position, the pressure came off his leg. James descended the slope quickly, followed sheepishly by the leader of the Peruvian rescuers.

"Barry, I think you'd better join me for the rest of the lowers. I should never have let our friend here work the ropes." James was frustrated with the Peruvian who had let a backup knot slide into the anchor and get hopelessly jammed. The Peruvians had wanted to run the whole rescue operation and had been offended when we had taken charge. For political reasons we had tried to allow the Peruvians to do as much as possible, but it was becoming obvious that their experience level with a technical rescue wasn't proficient enough for them to participate. We appreciated their good intentions, but Rob's safety and comfort were paramount.

The rest of the descent went smoothly. It was a long way, however, and by the time we reached the toe of the moraine, it was already 6:30 p.m. In half an hour it would be dark. We would have to set up camp. Michael arrived from our advance base camp with food and fuel, and dinner was prepared. James scouted a landing site for the helicopter, and we bivouacked for the night, hoping that Rob's painful ordeal would soon be over.

Kevin and Liz awoke well before dawn on June 8 and ascended the scree and boulders of the Valley of Death to our camp. It was Kevin's fourth trip, and he earned the nickname "Elevator Haberl." Rob had slept well and we felt confident that the helicopter would make it this time. The weather was clear, we were on the Santa Cruz side of the ridge, and we were 300 meters lower than the previous

146

It took incredible teamwork to lower, drag, and carry Rob down the rocky slabs and moraines of the Valley of Death. Alpamayo rises in the background.

day. As well, we now knew that the helicopter was a Bell 214 – a powerful machine able to operate at these altitudes.

At 8:00 a.m. we heard the thumping of the helicopter coming up the valley. It landed in the green meadow, and the first question from the pilot was: "Where are they?" Vicki explained that we had worked until dark moving Rob to the toe of the glacier but could go no farther. Vicki did her best to convince him, telling him that he was indeed a Spanish hero and that Rob was only 800 meters above the meadow.

Maybe they thought we hadn't really tried to get Rob closer. Most likely the pilot was simply making the right judgment based on his experience and level of skill flying in the mountains. After a short deliberation with his copilot, he refused. Magnanimously, though, he agreed to wait.

There were no more options. We had now been joined by four British climbers who had woken at dawn to carry a load of equipment and offer their services, and eight Americans from a guided trip who had spent the night with us at the toe of the glacier.

We had run out of snow to slide on, and it took all of our effort and energy to carry Rob over the steep, loose slope of rock and boulders. Our group worked well together – 22 people from four different countries. Slowly we moved down, passing Rob in the stretcher from one set of hands to the next over the steeper steps, carrying him cautiously in teams of 10 when the terrain allowed. Rob always claimed that the ride was comfortable.

It took four hours of hard work to reach the flats. The Peruvians, who had been tireless, suddenly became assertive, and four of them took over. Pushing their way to each corner of the stretcher, they began to carry Rob across the meadow at a trot. At first we were perplexed. Why the spontaneous and aggressive burst of energy? The appearance of a cameraman answered our question. Clearly it was some kind of macho display for television. We were indifferent, happy to let them have their moment in the spotlight, but Rob was definitely being jostled unnecessarily, so we stepped in and deliberately slowed the pace.

As we arrived at the helicopter, the pilot fired his machine. He was anxious to go even though there was no threat of poor weather or darkness. It was just before noon. Peter and Matt had decided to join Rob and Dave on the flight out of the mountains. All their gear was ready to go. We said our goodbyes as the rotor blades gained momentum.

"We need Rob's passport and airline ticket," Michael said, realizing that Rob's personal effects were still at the advance base camp tents. He ran to get them while James, weary of Peruvian logic, tried to explain the situation to the pilot. The copilot pointed to his watch and shouted, "No gas!" He slammed his door and the engine noise intensified, indicating the Peruvians' readiness to depart.

The helicopter roared and lifted slowly off the ground. Then, his head bobbing through the tall grass, Michael sprinted into the wind under the turning blades carrying a small bag. The pilot gave in and settled his machine back to earth.

James approached the helicopter as Michael hopped on board. "I'm going out with Rob!" Michael yelled into his ear so he could be heard over the howl of the engines. "He'll need someone to accompany him on the flight to Canada."

James just smiled and gave Michael the thumbs-up.

The door closed for the final time. The helicopter rose over the meadow, turned smoothly in a hover, then sped down the valley.

It was over.

Rob is loaded into the back of a Peruvian Military Bell 214. As the helicopter prepares for takeoff, Matt, Peter, and Michael also climb on board. Next stop for our injured friends is Lima, then home to Canada. Photo: Vicki Haberl.

149

AFTERWORD

THE FULL MOON WAS DAZZLING. I leaned across the bergschrund and hammered my tools into the vertical ice. Confident that both were secure, I committed to the route by shifting my weight to the front points of my crampons. After I had made a couple of moves on the sheer wall, the weight of the rope dangling between my legs tugged on my harness. It felt great to be climbing. I looked down and saw Kevin huddled against the bitter cold, feeding rope slowly through his belay as I moved upward. The brightness of the moon lit our way.

"On belay. Climb when ready." We used standard communication only. Every movement became a function of economy. My anchor was solid at the top on the first pitch. The angle had eased after the initial moves, and a full rope length up the steep Southwest Face was behind me. It was well before dawn on June 10. My mind flashed back to how we had come to be here.

AFTER THE HELICOPTER left the Quebrada Santa Cruz, everyone who had helped with the rescue shared a huge lunch. Then we slept. The next day in Lima, June 9, Rob, with Michael accompanying him, was sent by jet to Canada to have his leg set in a Toronto hospital. Peter was given the okay by the doctor in Lima and began the return journey to Huaráz. Matt had been let off the helicopter the day before in Huaráz and waited with a bruised hip and sore eyes for us to return from the mountains. In time, all his physical wounds would heal.

Back at our advanced base camp the remainder of the team, except for James, Barry, Kevin, and myself, packed up and left for Cashapampa. The four of us had

Alpenglow on the beautifully fluted Southwest
Face of Alpamayo.

to climb once more to the col camp to recover the remaining gear. None of us were enthusiastic; we were all very tired. Plodding up the Valley of Death was the last thing we wanted to do.

We reached the col in the middle of the afternoon. The weather was brilliant. We loitered on our packs, brewed tea, and discussed whether we should return to the valley right away or spend the night.

"What about Alpamayo?" Kevin said rhetorically.

"I'd still love to climb it," I ventured. "Do you think we should, though?" I wondered about the rest of the group. Given the events of the past few days, they would worry if we were late.

James had already calculated the timetable in his head. "If we get an early enough start, we could climb the face and be well on our way down the Santa Cruz by tomorrow night. We would be in Huaráz the following day. On schedule."

"It'll be a long day tomorrow, but I'm in," Barry added, making it a foursome.

Using the remainder of the afternoon to rest and recover, we drank as much fluid as we could and ate heartily. Our discussions centered around the proposed plan for the next day, and we took care to analyze both the weather and the potential hazard of the snow condition. All of us spoke openly about the accident and our rescue effort, reviewing both our mistakes and our many correct decisions. This sharing of perspectives, our first real opportunity to look back at it all, was an important process of reflection before committing to another climb.

As I lay in my sleeping bag that night, I thought about the ordeal we had undergone and examined my reasons for embarking so soon on a climb of Alpamayo. There were risks in climbing mountains. Even though we sometimes denied it, that fact had never been clearer than during the past five days. Our recent experience served as a reminder of the need to be objective and analytical in the mountains. More often than not, it seems, mountaineering becomes a passion. And passion, although a dynamic and powerful human quality whose energy can create masterful strokes of achievement, can just as easily cloud judgment.

Mountains are unforgiving. They don't care about the individual. Set in the harshest environments on the planet, mountains are sculpted by nature using various qualities of rock, ice, and snow. History has repeatedly shown that they don't tolerate reckless ambition or carelessness.

So why climb a mountain? I will never be able to express clearly an answer to satisfy that classic question. Probably no one will. It is too personal. But, as I lay there thinking about what had actually happened to us – the incredible response to a crisis, the competence and composure of my friends – it made me proud to have been part of such a qualified and caring group of people. The one common denominator among us was our love of the mountains and mountaineering. All of us were willing to test ourselves in a demanding environment where not everything was totally certain. That was a huge part of the attraction. Climbing was our path to experiencing life. For others it might be the love of music, the intensity of business, or any one of countless other passions that exist in our world. I knew I was lucky to have felt such a yearning and to have been able to pursue it, and I fell asleep eager for the alarm to ring.

Now, Kevin and I were leapfrogging pitches up the steep ice, concentrating on the climbing while the bright sphere of the full moon dropped toward the western horizon and began to compress into an oval. We stopped moving and stared as it changed from white to yellow, then to a soft orange glow as it neared the skyline. Just as the moon was about to vanish, it transformed magically into a fiery red ball. I had never seen anything like it. The sight was spellbinding. Then, too quickly, the vision slipped away and our attention was forced to return to the cold blue ice.

The night became dark.

With each swing our tools set firmly, easily. Our crampons were secure with a single kick. Kevin reached the ice ledge I had carved out of the face and took the lead. As the sky grew slowly brighter and the stars began to fade, I figured we would make the top in one more rope length. The cold air gnawed through my layers of clothing as I waited.

The rope payed out smoothly. Kevin was climbing quickly and would soon be up. Tiny ice particles ricocheted down the gully and bounced off my parka. When the rope went taut, I knew it was my turn.

I started toward the top. It was difficult to grip the tools with my icy fingers. The steady upward movement brought pain at first, then a welcome sensation of warmth. My heart pounded with the effort, but my body felt fit and acclimatized. Each breath was cool and fresh. There was nowhere I would rather have been. The climbing was challenging and superb, and I was sharing it with my best friend and brother.

The rope led over the top of the face into the sunshine. I shoved my ice ax into the flat snow on the ridge, hauled on the placement, and stood up. The sun was warm and the view of snowcapped peaks in every direction was endless. Kevin stopped pulling in the rope as I stepped toward him. We hugged.

Alpamayo.

Jim and Kevin Haberl on the summit of Alpamayo. Photo: James Blench

Glossary

ACUTE MOUNTAIN SICKNESS: a physiological response to hypoxia (a deficiency of oxygen reaching the tissues of the body) that is a product of high altitude. Symptoms include headache, insomnia, weakness, loss of appetite, and nausea.

AID-CLIMBING: climbing steep rock or ice walls by hanging on one piece of equipment (see protection) in order to place another, then moving up the wall by hanging on that piece. The process is repeated until that section of terrain is overcome.

ALPINE: the mountainous region above the tree line.

ANCHOR: the point at which the rope is secured – at the end of a pitch of climbing or for a rappel.

ASCENDER: a mechanical device that allows the climber to ascend a rope directly.

BELAY: a technique in which the rope between climbing partners is payed out or brought in to safeguard each other in the event of a fall.

BERGSCHRUND: the highest crevasse, separating the glacier below from the ice or snow wall above. Often a challenging obstacle, impeding access to the steep face of a mountain.

BIVOUAC: a night spent on a mountain or climb.

BUTTRESS: a prominent rocky feature that sticks out from the side of a mountain.

CAM OR CAMMING UNIT: a mechanical device used in the cracks of rock for protection.

CEREBRAL EDEMA: the swelling of the brain due to hypoxia (see Acute Mountain Sickness). In climbing it is usually the result of exposure to high altitude.

CLIMBING SKINS: synthetic attachments for the base of skis that allow grip in one direction and glide in the other. Used for climbing, then removed for a ski descent.

COL: a dip or saddle in a mountain ridge, often between two peaks. A high mountain pass.

COULOIR: a steep snow or ice gully on a mountainside.

CRAMPON: a close-fitting metal spike frame on a climber's boot that allows secure movement on hard snow and ice.

CREVASSE: a deep crack in glacial ice caused by the slow movement of the ice over irregular terrain features beneath the glacier.

DESCENDER: a metal friction device used for rappelling.

DOUBLE BOOT: a climbing boot with a plastic shell and an insulated inner boot for use in cold climates.

EXPANSION BOLT: a steel stud drilled into the rock, used for protection where cracks aren't available.

FALL LINE: a skiing term used to describe the path on a slope where gravity would cause a ball to roll. Usually it provides the best skiing.

FREE-CLIMBING: a type of climbing in which the climber ascends the rock face of a mountain using only hands and feet to move up. Protection equipment is used as a safeguard in the event of a fall. See aid-climbing.

ICE AX: a mountaineering tool used for climbing snow and ice, with a curved pick and an adze at one end of the shaft and a spike at the other end.

ICEFIELD: a large body of glacial ice with glacial tongues flowing out from the central mass.

ICE SCREW: a threaded metal tube that screws into ice and acts as protection for the climber.

JUMAR: see ascender.

LEAD: see pitch.

PITCH: a section of a climb, usually no more than the length of a standard climbing rope (50 meters).

PITON: a steel blade, in various shapes and sizes, that is hammered into a crack in the rock and used for protection.

PROTECTION: equipment placed in rock, snow, or ice for safety during a climb.

RAPPEL: a means of descent by sliding down a rope using a descender.

SUBALPINE: the mountainous region below the tree line.

TRAVERSE: a series of sideways moves; a horizontal section of climbing.

VERGLAS: a thin film of ice that often covers rock; it makes climbing difficult and dangerous and usually requires the climber to use crampons.